Teaching
With Writing

Teaching
With Writing

Toby Fulwiler

BOYNTON/COOK PUBLISHERS, INC.
UPPER MONTCLAIR, NEW JERSEY 07043

Library of Congress Cataloging-in-Publication Data

Fulwiler, Toby, 1942–
    Teaching with writing.

    References: pp. 155–158.
    1. English language—Rhetoric—Study and teaching.
2. English language—Composition and exercises.
3. Language arts—Correlation with content subjects.
4. Teachers' workshops.   I. Title.
LB2365.E5F85   1986   428'.007   86–14732
ISBN 0–86709–055–3

For information address Boynton/Cook Publishers, Inc.
52 Upper Montclair Plaza, P.O. Box 860, Upper Montclair, NJ 07043

Printed in the United States of America.

87   88   89   90   91   9   8   7   6   5   4   3   2   1

Acknowledgments

I want to thank all of my workshop co-leaders, who over the last ten years helped me develop the approach to language and learning represented in this book: at Michigan Tech these included Robert Jones, Randall Freisinger, Peter Schiff, Elizabeth Flynn, Art Young, and the late Bruce Petersen. At the University of Vermont these include Mary Jane Dickerson, Anthony Magistrale, Robyn Warhol, Arthur Biddle, Henry Steffens, and Michael Strauss. Thanks to Lee Odell and Dixie Goswami, who taught me to teach workshop style. Thanks to Bob Boynton for encouraging the project in the first place and to Peter Stillman for taming (somewhat) my talky voice. And thanks to Laura, Megan, and Anna who gave me the time to write over the five years this book was in the making.

Contents

Introduction

This book is written to clarify how writing across the curriculum improves learning across the curriculum. I first learned about this writing movement when I attended a National Endowment for the Humanities seminar at Rutgers in 1977. Seminar leaders Dixie Goswami and Lee Odell introduced me to the work of James Britton, James Moffett, Ken Macrorie, Peter Elbow, Janet Emig, James Kinneavy, and Mina Shaughnessy—among others—and I recall the distinct feeling of scales having fallen from my eyes; only three years earlier, I had completed a Ph.D. in English at a major research university and had never heard of such things as serious research and scholarship about the teaching of writing.

That fall, when I returned to direct the freshman writing program at Michigan Tech, I began working with my department head, Art Young, to develop a college-level program to promote more writing in all disciplines. We began, with virtually no funding, to offer two-day, off-campus workshops for our colleagues in history, business, and engineering; later, with a grant from General Motors, we expanded these workshops to four days and offered stipends to attending teachers. The workshop program proved successful. We were able to help our colleagues introduce more writing into their teaching and have a good time doing so.

But the workshops had perhaps an even greater effect on those of us directing them, as we realized how much more than "just writing" our program addressed. First, the workshops brought together faculty from diverse disciplines to talk about a common interest and thereby tapped a deeply felt need for more interaction and coherence in the university community. Second, the workshop modeled classroom pedagogy and so became for many professors a first conscious introduction to new teaching techniques. Finally, the workshop discussions refused to focus on skills alone—the subject most faculty thought they had come to master—but continued to explore the relationship between writing and thinking, learning, knowing, and caring, the whole business of education. In other words, the workshops reintroduced many to the very reasons we had become teachers in the first place.

Since 1977, I have conducted interdisciplinary writing workshops for elementary, secondary, and college teachers at different locations around the country. Since 1983, I have taught at the University of Vermont, again with faculty across the curriculum. Wherever I go, I continue to find serious interest among teachers to explore the role of written language in the larger educational process. In addition, the workshops have continued my own education: we who teach have so many common concerns, interests, and values. Yet, we have too few formats designed to help us share that commonness.

This book attempts to replicate—especially for secondary and college teachers who are not writing specialists—some of the ideas and issues with which writing workshops are concerned: how to improve the thinking and learning that goes on in the name of education.

I can't, of course, duplicate herein the intellectual and emotional electricity that comes with the workshop territory—to get that you'll have to attend one. But, where possible, I've let workshop participants add their own discoveries and have also tried to include some of the flavor of workshops by inviting you to participate, as you read, in the activity of journal writing, which both participants and leaders do with great frequency in actual workshop settings. Along the way, I've tried to document the best sources for this or that idea—but the more I've worked with composition pedagogy over the last nine years, the less sure I've become about whose ideas, exactly, I'm borrowing when. So far the field of teaching writing has proved remarkably free of territoriality when it comes to sharing ideas; I hope in this book to continue that tradition. Thus, you are encouraged to borrow as much or as little of the material as you like.

This book may prove especially useful for teachers who want an overview of the current state of writing instruction as it applies to teaching in the content area. Each chapter contains practical ideas for using writing in the classroom, together with some discussion of the theories on which those ideas are based. Furthermore, in keeping with the hands-on nature of the book, there's a section of workshop materials set off at the end of every chapter—invitations to journal write, workshop exercises, handouts and worksheets, and teacher and student responses to workshop experiences. Figure on writing your way through this book.

Before you begin any chapter, read the Pre-Chapter Journal Writing found at the end of the chapter.

Teaching with Writing may also have value for those who want to focus on particular topics like journals or research writing; each chapter stands fairly well by itself as an independent essay. Finally, I've arranged the topics in the same order as I would discuss them at an interdisciplinary writing workshop; workshop leaders may therefore find this a reasonable guide to read along with colleagues from many disciplines.

Toby Fulwiler
Essex Junction, VT

To all teachers who write
and all writers who teach.

1

Writing and Learning

BACK TO BASICS

Of the three Rs, the role of writing in learning—and in the school curriculum—is perhaps least understood. Nearly everyone believes that reading is *the* basic skill; without it few avenues to civilized culture or higher knowledge exist. There is a like conviction about mathematical languages: they are the foundation on which scientific and technical knowledge—and hence our civilization—is built. What *isn't* generally acknowledged is that writing is basic to thinking about, and learning, knowledge *in all fields* as well as to communicating that knowledge.

The emphasis on teaching reading in the elementary school curriculum may actually contribute to writing's neglect. Many American educators continue to teach to the model that puts reading before writing in the development of language-using skills, a hierarchy that actually separates reading from writing. Schools that subscribe to such an artificial hierarchy are also likely to subscribe to a set of basal readers accompanied by fill-in-the-blanks workbooks, which diminish the amount of writing a teacher is likely to assign in connection with the reading lesson. Donald Graves (1978) even suggests that the dominance of reading in the curriculum discourages active self-sponsored learning: "Writing is the basic stuff of education. It has been sorely neglected in our schools. We have substituted the passive reception of information for the active expressions of facts, ideas and feelings. We now need to right the balance between sending and receiving. We need to let them write."

Graves's position—that reading and writing are oppositely passive and active—is extreme. Frank Smith (1971), Kenneth Goodman (1968), and David Bleich (1978), among others, have

Reprinted, with changes, from *Fforum: Essays on Theory and Practice in the Teaching of Writing*, ed. by Patricia L. Stock (Upper Montclair, NJ: Boynton/Cook, 1983).

demonstrated that reading is a highly subjective and active process—hardly the passive activity which Graves describes. Each of us "reads" information differently because we have experienced the world differently. However, there remains enough truth in this observation to consider it further. In a sense, reading is the corollary opposite of writing: readers (listeners too) take in language from "outside" and process it through an internal mechanism colored by personal knowledge and experience to arrive at meaning. Writers, on the contrary, produce language from some internal mechanism, which is also shaped by personal knowledge and experience from "outside," to create meaning. So, just as no reader reads texts exactly the same way as other readers, no writer generates texts which are totally unique and original.

The importance in these qualified comparisons between reading and writing is this: they are interdependent, mutually supportive skills, both of which are basic to an individual's capacity to generate critical, independent thinking. Few courses of study, however, in the secondary schools or colleges, seem to recognize this relationship. Whereas reading is assigned in virtually every academic area as the best way to impart information, introduce ideas, and teach concepts, no such imperative exists regarding writing. In many subject areas, teachers are more likely to assign machine-scored short-answer, multiple-choice, and true-false tests than significant written responses. In fact, in a recent study of the writing required across the curriculum in American secondary schools, Arthur Applebee (1981) discovered that only three percent of assigned writing tasks required students to compose anything longer than a sentence; most of their so-called writing was "mechanical"—filling in blanks, copying, and doing homework exercises. Other courses may assign periodic essay tests, term papers, or laboratory reports, but use them to measure rather than promote learning.

A recent publication of the American Association for the Advancement of the Humanities (1982) reports findings similar to the Applebee study. The report says in part:

> Plainly, schooling as usual won't work. Most schools have a powerful hidden curriculum that precludes the development of higher-order skills in reading, thinking, and writing. The elements of this pernicious curriculum include the following:
>
> • No writing in the testing program, only short-answer, true-false, and multiple-choice tests.
> • Writing relegated only to English courses.

- Writing viewed as an end, not as a means, of learning.
- No systematic instruction in solving problems, thinking critically, and examining evidence.
- No opportunities for disciplined discussion in small groups.
- No regular practice in writing at length.

Not only is the curriculum pernicious, but teachers are seldom trained to understand fully the degree to which language skills are involved in the development of higher thought. The report continues:

> Moreover, most teachers are unprepared by their education or professional training to teach and foster the needed skills, just as most schools offer no in-service training for teachers and no small classes, released time, or teacher aides to help evaluate student writing.

These studies suggest that writing has an ill-defined and haphazard role in the curriculum. And even where writing has an established role, it is likely to be a superficial or limited one. If we are interested in helping both secondary schools and colleges do better what they are charged with doing—teaching people to reason systematically, logically, and critically—then we need to balance the curriculum as carefully with regard to writing activities as we currently do with reading activities. Moreover, the curriculum should not include merely *more* writing, but more of certain *kinds* of writing.

THOUGHT AND LANGUAGE

Over thirty years ago George Gusdorf (1977) stated clearly the double and often contradictory role language plays in individual development. On the one hand, humans use language to communicate ideas and information to other people; on the other, humans use language to express themselves and to develop their own articulate thought. These two functions, the "communicative" and the "expressive," often oppose each other; as Gusdorf puts it: "The more I communicate, the less I express myself; the more I express myself, the less I communicate."

Whereas Gusdorf's formulation of the double role of language may seem obvious and common-sensical, it is surprising to see the degree to which schools promote the "communicative," and neglect the "expressive." Most writing assigned in most curricula asks students to write to communicate learned information to teachers, through which writing the students will be evaluated, judged, and graded. Few curricula recognize, implicitly or explicitly, that writing can have an equally important role in generating knowledge (the expressive function) as in communicating it. In other words, an individual's language is crucial in discovering, creating, and formulating ideas as well as in communicating their substance to others.

Why am I making such an issue about the different functions of writing? Because I believe with James Britton that "knowledge is a process of knowing rather than a storehouse of the known." Much of the "process of knowing" takes place through language. Not only is it the symbol system through which we receive and transmit most information; it is the necessary medium in which we process or assimilate that information. We see and hear language, use it to explain experience, to identify the world. Gusdorf says: "To name is to call into existence, to draw out of nothingness. That which is not named cannot exist in any possible way." By naming objects and experience, we represent our world through symbols. Susanne Langer (1960) describes sensory data—what we take in from outside—as "constantly wrought into symbols, which are elementary ideas." To think in the first place, human beings need to symbolize, for in using language they represent, come to know, and understand the world. We actually do much of our learning through *making* language; or, another way, *language makes thinking and learning possible.*

For us, the process by which we think and learn is most important. Psychologist Lev Vygotsky (1962) describes "inner speech" as the mediator between thought and language, portraying it as a "dynamic, shifting, unstable thing, fluttering between word and thought." He argues that "thought is born through words . . . thought unembodied in words remains a shadow." (Sensory experience—sights, sounds, smells, tastes, touches—contributes to, but does not in itself constitute, formal thought.) We often think things through by talking to ourselves, carrying on inner conversations in which we consider, accept, reject, debate, and rationalize. The key to knowing and understanding lies in our ability to internally manipulate information and ideas received whole from external sources and give them verbal shape or *articulation*, which Richard Bailey (1983) defines as forming "sensory impressions and inchoate ideas into linguistic form." We think by processing; we process by talking to ourselves and others.

This last point is most important: we often inform ourselves by speaking aloud to others. Drawing on the work of Gusdorf, Langer, and Vygotsky, James Britton (1970a) argues that the "primary task for speech is to symbolize reality: we symbolize reality in order to handle it." Considered this way, speech serves the needs of the speaker as much as the listener. Britton argues that human beings use "expressive" speech—or talk—more to shape their own experience than to communicate to others: the words give concrete form to thought and so make it more real. This "shaping at the point of utterance" (Britton, 1982) helps us discover the meaning (our own meaning) of our everyday experience. As Martin Nystrand (1977) summarizes: language "facilitates discovery by crystallizing experience."

We carry on conversations with others to explain things to ourselves. I explain to a friend the symbolism in a Bergman film to better understand it myself. I discuss with my wife the gossip from a recent dinner party to give shape to my own perceptions of what occurred. And so on. The intersection between articulate speech and internal symbolization produces comprehensible meaning. This same intersection helps explain the role of writing in learning.

Many teachers identify writing simply as a technical communication skill necessary for the clear transmission of knowledge. This limited understanding of writing takes no account of the process we call "composing," the mental activity which characterizes our species. Ann Berthoff (1978) describes composing as the essence of thinking: "The work of the active mind is seeing relationships, finding forms, making meanings: when we write, we are doing in a particular way what we are already doing when we make sense of the world. We are composers by virtue of being human." Janet Emig (1977) believes that writing "represents a unique mode of learning—not merely valuable, not merely special, but unique." The act of writing, according to Emig, allows the writer to manipulate thought in unique ways because writing makes our thoughts visible and concrete and allows us to interact with and modify them. Writing one word, one sentence, one paragraph suggests still other words, sentences, and paragraphs. Both Berthoff and Emig point out that writing progresses as an act of discovery—and furthermore, that no other thinking process helps us develop a line of inquiry or a mode of thought as completely. Scientists, artists, mathematicians, lawyers, engineers—all "think" with pen to paper, chalk to blackboard, hands on terminal keys. For most of us, developed thinking is seldom possible any other way. We can hold only so many thoughts at one time; when we enter into dialogues with others or ourselves, we lose much of what we say because it isn't written down. More importantly, we can't extend, expand, or develop our ideas fully because we can't *see* them. Sartre quit writing when he lost his sight because he couldn't see words, the symbols of thought; he needed to visualize thought to compose, manipulate, and develop it (Emig, 1977).

SCHOOL WRITING

In 1975, James Britton and a team of researchers published a study of the kind of writing assigned to students 11 to 18 years old in British schools. The results of the study are not surprising: "transactional writing" (writing to communicate information) accounted for 64 percent of the total required writing. "Poetic writing" (writing as creative art) accounted for 18 percent—exclusively in English classes—while "expressive writing" (thoughts written to oneself) barely showed up at all, just 6 percent of the sample (Britton, 1975). Miscellaneous writing, including copying and note-taking, accounted for the rest. The figures are even more extreme in reference to writing assigned to 18-year-olds alone: transactional, 84 percent; poetic, 7 percent; and expressive, 4 percent.

The fact that students were seldom required to write in the expressive mode suggested to Britton that writing was taught almost exclusively as a means to communicate information rather than as a means to gain insight, develop ideas, or solve problems. This near-complete neglect of expressive writing across the curriculum is a clue to the perceived value of writing in schools. According to Britton's classification, which closely parallels Gusdorf's identification of the dual function of language, expressive writing is the most personal, the closest to "inner speech" and the thinking process itself.

The absence of assigned expressive writing in school curricula suggests that many teachers have a limited understanding of the way language works. As Britton's co-researcher Nancy Martin (1976) explains: "The expressive is basic. Expressive speech is how we communicate with each other most of the time and expressive writing, being the form of writing nearest speech, is crucial for trying out and coming to terms with new ideas." According to the research team, personal or expressive writing is the matrix from which both transactional and poetic writing evolve. Serious writers who undertake significant writing tasks almost naturally put their writing through "expressive stages as they go about finding out exactly what they believe and what they want to write" (Martin, 1976). Donald Murray (1978) explains: "I believe increasingly that the process of discovery, of using language to *find out what you're going to say*, is a key part of the writing process" (italics mine).

Preliminary findings in Applebee's 1981 study of writing in American schools indicate a pattern similar to the 1967–70 British study (Britton, 1975); "informational" (transactional) writing dominated the composing tasks in all disciplines; "imaginative" (poetic) writing was limited largely to English classes; "personal" (expressive) writing was virtually nonexistent in the sample. Applebee examines one additional category, "mechanical writing," which the Britton study did not consider in detail; Applebee describes it as any writing activity which did not involve significant composing on the part of the writer—filling in blanks, translating, computing, copying, taking notes, etc. This category, it turns out, was by far the most frequently assigned writing in American classrooms and accounted for 24 percent of total classroom activity (Applebee, 1981).

These studies suggest the kind of writing currently assigned by most teachers and written by most students in the junior and senior high school years. Transactional (or informational or communicative) writing dominates the curriculum while there is little or no evidence of expressive (or personal) writing. The pattern is a disturbing one, for it suggests that across the curriculum, from subject to subject, writing serves a narrow function. In fact, mechanical writing, in which students don't have to originate or develop thought to any significant extent, is the most frequently assigned form. Transactional writing, the only writing of paragraph length or longer assigned in most disciplines, communicates information, but usually to an audience already familiar with that information, who will evaluate or grade the writing—hardly an authentic act of communication. As Richard Bailey (1983) concludes: "the emphasis on writing as a tool for inquiry, a stage in the articulation of knowledge, seems so rare in American schools that it plays a negligible role in the educational system, at least at the secondary level."

WRITING ACROSS THE CURRICULUM

Schools exist primarily to teach people basic literacy skills which are prerequisites for learning basic thinking skills, which are in turn prerequisites for civilized existence as we know it. If we want schools to do more than teach the basics of thinking—if, in addition, we want schools to teach *critical, independent* thinking—then we must question the ill-defined role of writing throughout the curriculum. Brazilian educator Paulo Freire (1970) contends that "liberating education" only occurs when people develop their critical reasoning skills, including self-knowledge and self-awareness. This ability to think critically separates the autonomous, independent people, who are capable of making free choices, from the passive receivers of information. In Freire's terms, liberating education consists of "acts of cognition, not transferrals in information" (p. 67).

While it may be true that schools exist essentially to teach thinking, it is also true that many schools teach conformity and good manners and help justify the reigning political, social, and economic system. As a consequence, liberating education, as Freire describes it, is dangerous insofar as it aims to teach individuals to think autonomously, independently, and critically. Could it be that the lack of expressive writing in the curriculum reflects a lack of interest in critical thought? Or, worse still, are teachers afraid to teach their students to be free?

The Britton research team certainly entertained that possibility: "The small amount of speculative writing certainly suggests that, for whatever reason, curricular aims did not include the fostering of writing that reflects independent thinking; rather, attention was directed towards classificatory writing which reflects information in the form in which both teacher and textbook traditionally present it" (Britton, 1975). And former colleague Randall Freisinger (1982) gloomily insists that "Excessive reliance on the transactional function of language may be substantially responsible for our students' inability to think critically and independently. . . . Product-oriented, transactional language promotes closure."

But most of my colleagues in elementary or secondary school or in college don't *want* to promote "closure." They truly want to teach students to be free, autonomous thinkers. They simply don't realize the role writing can play in effecting this. At the same time, however, when I ask teachers from different disciplines to identify the student writing problems which bother them most, a few mention spelling, punctuation, or grammar, while the majority talk about problems related to flawed thinking: inability to focus, organize, write a thesis statement, develop a paragraph, use supporting evidence, cite references, etc. When Jack Meiland (1983) asked his colleagues at the University of Michigan the same question he reports similar answers: "The most frequent complaints were that students did not know how to develop their ideas and organize their ideas. They did not know how to formulate their ideas clearly, argue for their ideas, develop replies to possible objections, uncover hidden assumptions, discover the implications and consequences of a position, and so on." In other words, most teachers recognize that a fundamental writing-thinking connection exists, yet they seldom examine exactly what that connection is, how it works, and how it might inform their pedagogical practice. Meiland, who is aware of that connection, actually created a specific, specialized course in critical thinking, where students were "taught intellectual skills directly and explicitly." He suggests that the best way to teach such skills is to teach "the associated forms of writing. For example, I teach skills of argumentation by teaching students to write argumentative papers."

A more common variation of this "thinking skills course," which will improve writing along the way, is the writing course which aims to teach thinking along the way. One such course is offered by Peter Elbow (1983), who teaches his students to freewrite, brainstorm, and keep journals to explore and develop their thoughts through personal, private language. A much different approach to a similar end is that of Frank D'Angelo (1983), who teaches a highly structured writing course which emphasizes classical imitation. Here students first analyze, then imitate pieces of good writing to emulate "the best features of a writer's style." Such an exercise "mirrors the writer's cognitive processes, leading the student writer to a discovery of new effects." Finally, we might look at the approach advocated by William Coles (1983), who argues that writing must be taught as an avenue to power. "To become alive to the implications of language using is not, of course, to become free, but it is to have choices that one cannot have without such an awareness." Coles's approach stresses the value of language-using for writers—enabling them "to run orders through chaos, shape whatever worlds [they] live in, and as a consequence gain the identities [they] have." In other words, writing becomes synonymous with growing—the necessary precondition for autonomy and freedom.

But for such skill-specific courses to have a lasting, purposeful impact, the lessons they teach must be reinforced regularly, across the curriculum. Such courses work best with well-prepared, motivated students who are willing to treat seriously what are obviously "practice exercises"—a term used by both Meiland and D'Angelo. Many other students, still groping for a foothold in the academic or social world, simply may not be ready when such a course comes their way (or is required in their schedule). While good teachers, such as Meiland, Elbow, D'Angelo, and Coles, can help generate motivation where little existed before, such courses will not reach all students in all curricula.

A second approach, meant to have an impact on *all* students, asks that they learn writing and thinking skills in the context of their own career interests. Richard Ohmann (1976) writes: "People have concerns, needs, impulses to celebrate or condemn, to compact with others or to draw battle lines against them, to explain, appeal, exhort, justify, criticize. Such concerns, needs, and impulses are what lead people to write (and to speak) when they are not writing to measure." Students assigned to write "exercise" prose on academic topics to teachers who will "measure" them often do so in language which Ken Macrorie (1976) describes as "Engfish"— the stilted, evasive prose common to school and bureaucratic writing alike. Much poor writing—and poor thinking—according to Macrorie stems from students who "[have] spent too many hours in school mastering English and reading cues from teachers and textbooks that suggested it is the official language of the school. In it the student cannot express truths that count for him." Both Ohmann and Macrorie seek to develop intellectual skills within the context of the individual student's life and work. In other words, if we want writing (and thinking) skills to become useful, powerful tools among our students we must ask them to write (and think) in a context which demands some measure of *personal commitment*— which, in schools, is more likely to be in their major discipline than in specialized composition classes.

We know, of course, that the whole school environment influences how students learn to read, write, and think about the world. While individual teachers and particular classes may be the most memorable and visible aspects of education, the more covert structure of the curriculum also "teaches." Schools that offer most of their instruction through large classes, lectures, rote drills, and multiple-choice examinations obviously do little to nurture each student's individual voice. Schools that offer small classes, encourage student discussion, and assign frequent and serious compositions do nurture that voice.

According to *The Forum for Liberal Education*, numerous institutions of higher learning have "comprehensive writing programs" to improve both writing and learning skills *across the curriculum*: at Yale and the University of Michigan, for example, such programs are controlled by boards composed of interdisciplinary faculty concerned with school-wide policies on writing; at Beaver College, Michigan Tech, and the University of Vermont, faculty members attend writing workshops and learn to assign and evaluate writing more effectively in any academic discipline.

These programs are cited to emphasize a particular point: while the programs vary widely in size and scope, all assert that writing is a complex intellectual process central to both creative learning and proficient communication. They argue collectively that writing deserves serious reconsideration, increased attention, and ever more thoughtful practice—across the whole school curriculum.

The degree to which the curriculum promotes (demands?) comprehensive language activities on the part of students may be the degree to which it creates a genuinely liberating education. It is apparent that we need both pedagogical approaches described here: intensive writing/reasoning courses on the one hand and extensive reasoning/writing activities in all courses on the other. For this to happen consistently, more teachers in all disciplines need to study the several dimensions of language which most actively promote clear writing and critical reasoning.

When teachers across the curriculum reflect on "why we teach writing in the first place," their answers will be neither simple nor formulaic. Learning to write, like learning to learn, depends on a complex relationship between writer, subject and instruction. Writing and learning interlock, however, when teachers ask students to write in order to create, contemplate and act, as well as drill, copy and test. As James Moffett (1981) puts it: "Instead of using writing to test other subjects, we can elevate it to where it will *teach* other subjects, for in making sense the writer is making knowledge." Writing to make sense and knowledge is what this book is about.

WORKSHOP ACTIVITIES

Pre-Chapter Journal Writing

Before reading the chapter, take a few minutes and answer a few questions, in writing, which have a direct bearing on the reading which follows. A good way to read this or any book, of course, is to write as you read, both anticipating what is to come and reacting to what has just passed. In fact, journal writing is one of the key pedagogical techniques discussed, useful to faculty and students alike. I'll suggest some ideas for journal writing at the beginning and end of each chapter. Don't let them limit you; you may have better ones.

Consider the following questions:

1. List the different kinds of writing, both personal and professional, that you are likely to do in a given year.
2. Articulate several reasons why you write. Is one more important than the others?
3. What kind of writing gives you the greatest pleasure?

Post-Chapter Journal Writing

Write a paragraph in response to each of the following questions:

1. What kinds of writing do you ask your students to do?
2. Why do you ask them to write in these particular ways?
3. Which assignments do they seem to write best? (Do you know why?)

Workshop Exercise

Writing to Learn

One way to demonstrate the power of writing as a learning tool is to structure the first day of class around three brief assignments. Before your students have read anything about your subject—history, biology, business, or whatever—ask them to write in the following sequence:

1. Write everything you know about [course subject]. (10 minutes)

Ask for volunteers to read aloud what they have written; assure them that any response is OK. On the blackboard, make a list of topics that come up as people read. After 15 minutes, ask a second question.

2. Write about one item on the blackboard in as much detail as you can. (10 minutes)

Ask people about what they have written—encourage paraphrases this time rather than actual readings. Add to the discussion what you know that will enhance some of the ideas. After 15 minutes, ask one more question:

3. What questions do you have about any ideas which came up today?

Again make a list, etc. . . .

Workshop Handout

Two Roles of Expressive Writing

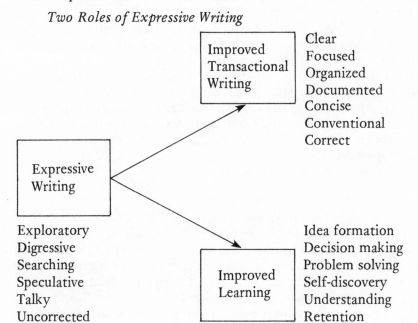

Expressive Writing

Improved Transactional Writing

Clear
Focused
Organized
Documented
Concise
Conventional
Correct

Exploratory
Digressive
Searching
Speculative
Talky
Uncorrected

Improved Learning

Idea formation
Decision making
Problem solving
Self-discovery
Understanding
Retention

Teachers Respond

Why Do You Write?

1.   I write because I like words. I don't think I could do it—even professionally—if I didn't like the exercise. It's too intensive and personal and it competes equally with my love of teaching. If I had to write and didn't like it, I'd just go off and teach all the time.

But it (writing) draws me because I love to try to catch at a thought and try to put it down. And I love to play with the sounds of thoughts. Sometimes, there's more than play—sometimes I just have to put an idea or a feeling down because I feel better for having done it or else I know that feeling will stay with me when it's written.

The other kind of writing is the required writing—lists, checks, memos. . . . I pay attention to the joy of the expression, I even like to write witty (or nasty) remarks on the line at the bottom of checks. And my lists resemble Gargantua's. Sometimes I add something whimsical to make me laugh in the midst of doing endless chores.

I think writing helps me sort things out.

2.   I write because I communicate best in writing—far better than by talking.

I have things I want to tell people: the results of research, views on how things ought to be run, helpful hints to students for writing papers and exams, how to study, etc.

I also write for myself, although often in a form that others will read, such as letters.

I write as a form of exercise, much as I run races, always seeking improvement. The rewriting is, for me, an end in itself in the same way that running a particular distance faster is a personal accomplishment.

(This would be vastly improved in a second draft.)

3.   I write for many reasons (purposes): for pleasure; to help "firm up" my thinking; to persuade other people; to explain something (to students, faculty, administrators); to request information; to defend myself; to help me remember; to get something published; to support/explain a position; to make something official (e.g., my signature on x); for the record—e.g., a memo "to the files"; to praise or thank someone; to reprimand someone; to share an experience; to recommend (a book, a movie, a person); *not* to recommend; to flatter; to thank; to request; to summarize (as on the blackboard); to make specific (syllabus, exam question); because, sometimes, I *have* to. I write because—in part—of the society we live in and my role in it.

2

Student Journals

Journal writing introduces students to expressive writing easily and systematically. In 1967, when I began teaching college English, I assigned journals in composition and literature courses, but used them sparingly in the classroom, preferring students to write on their own. Some students used them well, while most never really understood what kind of writing they were supposed to do in them. I no longer trust to chance; journals work now for most of my students because I use them actively every day to write in, read from, and talk about—in addition to whatever private writing the students do on their own. These everyday journal-writes replace other routine writing assignments, from pop quizzes to book reports. Journal writing in class stimulates classroom discussion, starts small group activity, clarifies hazy issues, reinforces learning, and stimulates imaginations.

Journal writing works because with every entry instruction is individualized; the act of silent writing, even for a few minutes, generates ideas, observations, emotions. It's hard to daydream, doze off, or fidget while one writes. Journal writing won't make passive students miraculously active learners; it does, however, make it harder for students to remain passive.

Teachers in all subject areas and grade levels find it easy to increase class writing by using journals. Regardless of class size, this kind of informal writing need not take more teacher time; journals can be spot checked, skimmed, read thoroughly, or not read at all, depending on the teacher's interest and purpose. Journals have proved to be remarkably flexible documents; some teachers call them "logs," others "commonplace books" or "day books," still others "idea notebooks." While I prefer students to keep looseleaf binders, science teachers (conscious of patent rights) often require bound notebooks. While I suggest pens (pencils smear), a forestry teacher suggests pencils (ink smears in the rain). And so on.

ACADEMIC JOURNALS

What does a journal look like? How often should people write in them? What kinds of writing should they do on their own? How should I grade them? These questions often occur to the teacher who has not used or kept journals before. Following are some possible answers.

Journals might be looked at as part diary and part class notebook: while diaries record the private thought and experience of the writer, class notebooks record the public thought and presentation of the teacher. The journal is somewhere between the two. Like the diary, the journal is written in the first person about ideas important to the writer; like the class notebook, the journal may focus on academic subjects the writer wishes to examine.

Diary ————————⟶ Journal ⟵———————— Class Notebook
(Subjective expression)   (I/it)   (Objective topics)

Journals may be focused narrowly on the subject matter of one discipline, or broadly on the whole range of a person's academic and personal experience. Each journal entry is a deliberate exercise in expansion: "How far can I take this idea? How accurately can I describe or explain it? How can I make it make sense to me?" The journal encourages writers to become conscious, through language, of what is happening to them, both personally and academically.

Student writers should be encouraged to experiment with their journals, to write often and regularly on a wide variety of topics, to take some risks with form, style, and voice. Students should notice how writing in the early morning differs from writing late at night. They might also experience how writing at the same time every day, regardless of inclination or mood, often produces surprising results. Above all else, journals are places where students can try out their expressive voices freely, without fear of evaluation. Students can write about academic problems and progress to sort out where they are, how they're doing and perhaps discuss what to do next. Teachers can ask students to engage in certain kinds of speculation in their journals and so plant seeds for class discussion and more formal writing projects.

JOURNAL ASSIGNMENTS

Journals record each student's personal, individual travel through the academic world and also serve as springboards for

formal writing assignments; they generate life and independent
thought in a sometimes over-formal classroom atmosphere. *Any*
assignment can be made richer by adding a written dimension
which encourages personal reflection and observation. Field notes
jotted in a biology notebook become an extended observation
written in a biology journal; this entry, in turn, might well become
the basis for a major research project. Personal reflections recorded
in a history journal can help the student identify with, and perhaps
make sense of, the otherwise distant and confusing past. Trial hypotheses might find first articulation in social science journals;
continued writing about strong ideas can develop those ideas into
full-fledged research designs and experiments. The suggestions
which follow might be useful in some of your classes:

Starting Class.   Introduce a class with a five-minute journal-
write. Any class. Any subject. In a discussion class, suggest a topic
related to the day's lesson (a quote from the reading assignment,
for instance), and allow those first few minutes for students to
compose (literally) their thoughts and focus them in a public direction; without that time, the initial discussion is often halting
and groping. After such a journal entry, the teacher may ask someone to read an entry aloud to start people talking. It is hard sometimes to read rapidly written words in public, but also rewarding
when the language generates a response from classmates. I often
read my own entry first to put students at ease, for my sentences
may be awkward, halting, and fragmentary just as theirs sometimes
are. Repeated periodically, this exercise provides students with a
structured oral entry into the difficult public arena of the classroom and helps affirm the value of their personal voice.

Like the discussion class, the lecture also benefits from a
transition exercise which starts students thinking about the sched-
uled topic. For example, prior to beginning a lecture in a nineteenth-century American literature class studying Transcendental-
ism, I often ask students to define their concept of romanticism in
their journals. I might then commence lecturing directly, using the
brief writing time to set the scene or mood for the lecture; or I
might start a short discussion based on the student writing as a
lead into the lecture. Either way, the students involve themselves
with the material because they have committed themselves,
through their own language, to at least a tentative exploration of
an idea.

Summarizing.   End a class with a journal-write. This exercise
asks students to summarize information or ideas they have learned
during class. The summary entry serves several purposes: to find

out what, if anything was learned today, and to find out what questions are still unanswered. These issues can be handled orally, of course, without a journal, but writing loose thoughts onto paper often generates tighter thinking. And again, private writing in a noisy, busy public forum allows the learner to collect thoughts otherwise lost in the push-and-shove hurry to leave class. Too often instructors lecture right to the bell, still trying to make one last point, while at the same time realizing by the rustle in the room that the students are already mentally on their way to lunch. Better, perhaps, to cover less lecture territory and to end class with students' own observations and summary in journals. That final act of writing/thinking helps students synthesize material for themselves and so increases its value.

Gary Johnson (1981), a teacher in the Fine Arts Department of Northern Kentucky University, uses journals at summary points in his music appreciation class. In describing how journals help his music students, Johnson makes a good case for students in all subject areas:

> In Music Appreciation, I found students were able to remember material presented in a lecture format if I assigned a timed write at the conclusion of an important articulation point in the lecture. In reading student-writes, it became evident that they were going far beyond the "lesson summary" use of the journal. The journal-write itself seemed to be an aid to comprehension. Students would often begin with "I really don't understand (such and such)" then, at some point, add, "I guess it means that . . ." or "It has something to do with . . ." Then the writes tended to step logically through the subject, ending with either a well-defined question for the instructor, or a comment that took the subject one step beyond the lecture. The journal-write seemed to force students to think through a topic and synthesize discrete facts into a logical framework for retention.

Teachers may also ask their students to summarize a given unit in a course, or the meaning of the whole course itself. Following is a journal entry written by a student at the end of a college American literature class:

> I suppose this will be the last entry I make in this journal, so I would like to sort of use this time to sum up my thoughts I have up to this point. So far, at least the first two authors we have to read have led tragic, unhappy lives. I wonder if this is just a coincidence or if it has something to do with the per-

sonality of a successful writer. I feel that through the use of
this journal over the weeks I have been able better to understand certain aspects of each story by actually writing down
what's bothering me, what I like, and what I don't. A lot of
thought has gone into the past pages, and that thought has
really contributed to making the class better. Many times I
didn't even realize that something bothered me about a story
until I put down my feelings in words. I wasn't even sure how
I even felt about The Sun Also Rises until I kicked a few
ideas around on paper. In short, this journal has been a useful tool in my understanding and appreciating this class.

[TOM K.]

Even as he writes about the value of the journal, Tom shows
us his speculative personal style with phrases like "I suppose" and
"I wonder." Reviewing his journal, the writer notes that his written observations about "what's bothering me" have helped him see
larger patterns. The very structure of the journal—sequential,
chronological, personal—provides the material from which generalizations and hypotheses can be made. The journal leads this student to wonder about the relationship between good writing and
"tragic, unhappy lives." In this manner, each individual act of
summary is potentially a discovery.

Focusing.   Structure a class through a journal-write. Plan a
five-minute writing task in the midst of the 50-minute class to give
focus to an idea or problem. Listening becomes passive and note-
taking often mechanical; even the best students drift into day-
dreams from time to time. A journal-write gives students a chance
to re-engage themselves personally with the class topic. Writing
changes the pace of the class; it shifts the learners into a partici-
pant role and sometimes forces clarity from confusion simply by
demanding that pen be put to paper. Writing clears out a little
space for students to interact with the ideas thrown at them and
allows them to focus problems while the stimulus is still fresh.
"Reflect on the notion that Karl Marx is a philosopher rather than
a scientist," or "Explain the phrase 'How do I know what I think
until I see what I say?' in your own language and make sense of
it." If planned in advance, these pauses can be both welcome
breaks and fruitful exercises.

In the middle of a class studying "scientific and technical
writing," I discovered a number of students who questioned the
idea that even technical writing was persuasive, depending on how
facts and information were presented, phrased or formatted. I

gave the class an impromptu journal assignment, asking them to write for five minutes on the thesis that "all writing is persuasive." Following is a sample response:

> "All Writing is Persuasive"—It's hard to write on my understanding of this quote because I don't think that all writing is persuasive. What about assemblies for models and cookbook recipes. I realize that for stories, newspaper articles, novels and so forth that they are persuasive. But is *all* writing persuasive? I imagine that for assemblies and so forth that they are persuading a person to do something a particular way. But is this really persuasive writing?
>
> [JIM S.]

By writing about their understanding of this idea, rather than just arguing back and forth in class, students were forced into a deeper, more thoughtful consideration of the proposition. Writing allowed them to test the idea in private, in conversations with themselves, and so made the ensuing public discussion more careful. This student, for example, begins by writing, "I don't think that all writing is persuasive," and concludes by recognizing that even in assembly instructions "they are persuading a person to do something a particular way." The writing has sharpened the focus of the learning.

A variation on the planned writing pause is the spontaneous one, where the teacher senses misunderstanding in the audience or where the teacher even loses track of an idea. While writing in journals, both teachers and students may refocus the problem and so make the next 15 or 20 minutes more profitable.

A digressive or rambling discussion may be refocused by simply calling time out and asking students to write for a few minutes in their journals: "What are we trying to explain?" or "Restate the argument in your own words; then let's start again." Pauses in a discussion change the class pace and allow quiet, personal reflection. Teachers can all use a little time out in some classes, yet seldom find a pedagogical justification for it. The journal-write is a good solution. In one-sided discussions, where a few students dominate and others can't participate, interrupt with a short writing task and sometimes the situation reverses itself, as the quiet ones find their voices while the loud ones cool off. The group also can become more conscious of the roles people play in class by asking questions like: "What is your part in this discussion?" or "Try to trace how we got from molecules to men in the last 15 minutes," or "Why do you think Sarah just said what she did?" Writing about talking provides distance and helps generate thoughts we didn't have before.

Problem Solving.   Use journals as a vehicle for posing and solving problems. In a class on modern literature, ask students to write about the lines in an E. E. Cummings poem which they don't understand; the following day many students will have written their way to understanding by forcing their confusion into sentences. What better way to make sense out of "what if a much of a which of a wind" or "my father moved through dooms of love"? Math or science teachers might ask their students to solve difficult equations by using j-writes when they are confused. For example, Margaret Watson (1980), a high school teacher from Oklahoma, reports that using journals in her mathematics classes has improved her students' ability to solve math problems. She asks students questions such as: "The problem I had completing a square was . . ." and "This is how to . . ." Watson reads the journals and comments to each student individually about his or her feelings about mathematics: "This two-way conversation has been beneficial to the class. The students realize I hear them and care. They seem to have looked inside themselves and to have seen what they could do to help their mathematical problems. Many of their grades improved."

The journal could become a regular tool in any subject area to assist students in solving problems since the act of writing out the problem is, itself, a clarifying experience. Switching from number symbols to word symbols sometimes makes a difference; putting someone else's problem into your own language makes it *your* problem and so leads you one step further toward solution. The key, in other words, is articulating to yourself what the problem is and what you might do about it. Following is a brief example of a student talking to himself about a writing block:

> I'm making this report a hell of a lot harder than it should be. I think my problem is I try to edit as I write. I think what I need to do is first get a basic outline of what I want to write then just write whatever I want. After I'm through, then edit and organize. It's hard for me though.
>
> [BRUCE M.]

Responding.   Use journals to sharpen student responses to their academic experience. Class discussions, teacher questions, books, movies, TV and music all provide material to be written about. Using the journal as the place to write their reactions to class material asks the students to go one step beyond vaguely

thinking about their responses—but stays short of making a formal
written assignment which might cause unproductive anxiety over
form or style. In some disciplines, like engineering, math, or
physics, such questions might be less "open-ended" than ones
asked in liberal arts courses, but even in the most specialized fields
some free, imaginative speculation helps—and when that speculation is recorded in the journal, students have a record to look at
later to show where they've been and perhaps suggest where to
go next.

Science and social science teachers might ask students to
keep a "lab journal" in addition to a lab notebook to record responses to their experiments. This adds a personal dimension to
keeping records and also provides a place to make connections
between one observation and the next. Perhaps journal entries
should be interleafed next to the recorded data. The same may be
done with a "field notebook" in biology or forestry: to the objective data add each student's own thoughts about that data. Such
personal observations might prove useful in writing a report or
suggest the germ for another paper or project.

A college political science professor uses journals for a variety
of homework assignments in his course, American Government and
Politics. He asks students to record frequently their opinions about
current events; he also requests them to write short personal sum-
maries of articles in their journals, thereby creating a sequential
critical record of readings accomplished during the term. While
both of these activities may be conducted through other written
forms, using the journal is simple and economical for both students
and teacher. In like manner, a high school teacher of remedial
English asks his students to practice writing about movies he shows
in class. The following entry was written in response to a science
fiction film:

> The movie was pretty good. It's weird how they could make a
> human out of that stuff and say they're a Robot. If people
> could change color I sure as hell wouldn't want to change.
> The movie was pretty shocking to me. I hope it really doesn't
> happen in the future. I really don't know how people could
> plug themselves in just to wake up, that's pretty dumb. It
> would be pretty decent to see Robots looking just like all of
> us though.
>
> [ANDREW M.]

This entry has the characteristic misspellings and awkward punctuation of a remedial tenth-grade writer; it also reveals some interesting thoughts which could contribute to both class discussion and a

future writing assignment. Here we have material to talk and write about further; the act of writing the response to the movie preserved and maybe even generated the thought.

In addition to responding to readings and movies, journals prove useful for highly subjective experiences such as listening to music. One of music teacher Gary Johnson's (1981) students, a physical education major, put it this way:

> There are times, when listening to a piece of music, that it "does something" to you. Music plays on your emotions. Many times it's difficult to interpret your emotions. It seems the easiest way would be writing them down.
>
> I find it helpful—because sometimes a work is so good (or so bad)—you have to get it out of your system. I also find journal writes helpful when I study for a test. At that moment you do a write you have more insight into it than you will a week later. A week later you may understand it better—but you won't have the initial insight you did at first.
>
> [SHARON L.]

Another music teacher asked her students to keep "listening journals" to record their daily experience of hearing music. Periodically, she conducted discussion classes which relied heavily on the subjective content of the journals and so involved the students both personally and critically in her course content. In similar fashion, a drama teacher currently asks his actors to keep a journal to develop more fully their awareness of a character or scene. He has found that his student actors work their way into their characters by writing out responses to various scenes, dialogues and dramatic events within the play.

Progress Reports. Use journals to monitor student progress through the class. Richard Heckel, a Michigan Tech metallurgy professor, has prepared a full-page handout with suggestions to students about using journals in Introduction to Materials Science. He uses journals to encourage thoughtful reflection upon important topics, to practice writing answers to possible exam questions, and to improve writing fluency. Specifically, he asks students to write about each day's lecture topic prior to attending class; after class, they are asked to write a summary or write questions about the lecture. Periodically, these journals are checked to monitor student progress through the course, but they are not graded. Heckel also monitors his own teaching through journals. In reading his first batch of 100 journals, he was surprised to discover few charts, diagrams or drawings among the student writing. Believing that metallurgical engineers must develop visualization skills to a high degree, he introduced a unit on visual thinking into his course. Here the journal indicated to him what was missing in the thinking processes of his students and so changed a part of his pedagogical approach.

Robert Stinson (1980), geography professor at Michigan Tech, has used journals for 10 years in large lecture classes. In Recreational Geography, he asks students to keep journals to stimulate their powers of observation. By requiring students to write down what they see, he finds that they look more closely and carefully and, hence, begin to acquire the rudimentary techniques of scientific observation. He also requires students in Conservation to keep journals; specifically, at the beginning of new course topics, he asks them to write definitions of terms or concepts which they misuse or misunderstand. At the conclusion of each topic, he requests another written definition to compare how their initial perceptions have changed. During the final week of the 10-week course, he asks students to compose an essay about their attitude changes toward conservation as a result of the course. The journal is the primary resource for this last assignment, revealing to both instructor and student what has been learned, what not.

I often ask students to make informal progress reports to themselves about what they are learning in class. I'm interested in having students share these thoughts with me and/or the class— volunteers often read passages aloud after such an assignment. But more important, I think, are the observations students make to themselves about what they are learning. My question is the catalyst, but the insights are only of real value if they are self-initiated. Following is a sample response from a student studying technical writing; he refers to an exercise in which the entire class "agreed" that one piece of writing was better than another:

> After, we took a vote and decided which proposal letter we liked the best—it really made me wonder. I hadn't realized it but we've been conditioned to look for certain things in this class. I guess that's the purpose of any class, strange how you don't notice it happening though.
>
> [ARNOLD S.]

Class Texts. Ask students to write to each other, informally, about concerns and questions raised in the class. By reading passages aloud, or reproducing passages to share with the class, students become more conscious of how their language affects people. First-year humanities students actually suggested that duplicated journal passages should become a part of the humanistic content of the course; we mimeographed selected journal entries, shared them for a week and all learned more about each other. Passing these journal-writes around class suggested new writing possibilities to the students; in this case, the stimulus to experiment came from classmates rather than teacher and so had the strong validity of peer education.

An entry such as the following, written about a geography class, can go a long way toward provoking classmates into a discussion of topical issues:

> I don't know if I'm just over-reacting to my Conservation class or not, but lately I've become suspicious of the air, water, and food around me. First we're taught about water pollution, and I find out that the Portage Canal merrily flowing right in front of my house is unfit for human contact because of the sewage treatment plant and how it overflows with every hard rain. Worse yet, I'm told raw sewage flows next to Bridge Street. I used to admire Douglas Houghton Falls for its natural beauty, now all I think of is, "That's raw untreated sewage flowing there."
>
> Our next topic was air pollution. Today I was informed that the rain here in the U. P. has acid levels ten times what it should, thanks to sulfur oxide pollution originating in Minneapolis and Duluth. I'm quite familiar back home in Ishpeming with orange birch trees due to iron ore pelletizing plants.
>
> Is there any escaping this all encompassing wave of pollution? I had thought the Copper Country was a refuge from the poisonous fact of pollution, but I guess its not just Detroit's problem anymore. As I write these words, in countless places around the globe, old Mother Nature is being raped in the foulest way. I get the feeling someday she'll retaliate and we'll deserve it. Every bit of it.
>
> [BILL W.]

An additional note about this entry: notice the number of references to local places (Portage Canal, Bridge Street, Douglas Houghton Falls); Bill doesn't bother to explain or identify these references because his writing is aimed at an audience familiar with the area about which he writes. Initially he writes to himself, but if he chooses later to share an entry with classmates, he can assume that they know the local areas as well as he does. Journal writing is characterized by this limited, closed context, in which the writer assumes his writing will not go far from his own person. To shape this piece for a larger audience would require explaining that these geographic sites are in and around Houghton, Michigan in the Upper Peninsula, etc. A beneficial corollary of writing to a limited audience is more frank, honest, and vulnerable writing; Bill trusts that this writing won't see large circulation and so feels freer to say more, take some risks, and write about what's really on his mind.

Records of Intellectual Growth. Journals have a signal value in preserving early thought and, at the same time, encouraging that thought to develop and change as the writer develops and changes. Consider the following fragments from Joan's journal, which show her progress through a summer course, Introduction to Philosophy. Joan, a senior, was required by her instructor to keep a journal and record her reactions to the class and to new ideas that she encountered during this five-week course. Here is an entry from early in her first week of class:

> This philosophy stuff is weird! Hard to conceptualize. You try to explain it to someone and just can't. Like taking 3 pages of the book to decide whether or not a bookcase is there. Someone asked me if you really learn anything from it. I didn't think so but I finally had to say yes. I really never realized how we speak without really knowing (??!) what we are saying. Like I told her, the class is interesting and time goes by fast in it but you have to concentrate and sort of "shift" your mind when you are in class. You have to really think and work hard at keeping everything tied in together— it's like a chain where you have to retain one thing to get the next. I also told her that if you really do think and concentrate you begin to agree with this guy on skepticism, etc. and that's *really* scary—you think at the end of that book will be this little paragraph saying how everything really does exist as we see it and we really do "know" things, they were just kidding!

At the beginning she wonders about the nature of her new course of study: "weird." She encounters Descartes for the first time and openly explores her thoughts on paper, hoping that his ideas are essentially a joke and that Descartes is "just kidding." Near the end of the course a month later, after much debate in her journal about her religious beliefs, she writes:

> You know, as the term is coming to a close I am tempted to sit back and think if I really mastered any skills in philosophy. Sometimes when I come up with arguments for something I feel like I am just talking in circles. Or "begging the question"

as it's been put. One thing I can say is that Philosophy has made somewhat of a skeptic out of me. We are presented with so many things that we take for granted as being there and being right—we were shown evidence and proofs that maybe they really aren't there and aren't true. You know, I still feel like I did the first entry I put in this journal—maybe the last day of class you will say—"I was just kidding about all this stuff—the world really is as you imagine it—there are material things, God does exist with evil, etc." But I realize these arguments are valid and do have their points—they are just points we never considered. I can see I will not take much more for granted anymore—I will try to form an argument in my mind (not brain!).

At this point we see her reflecting on her course of study, on her journal, and on how she has possibly changed. Joan remains a Christian—a belief she has asserted several times in her journal—but she now also calls herself "somewhat of a skeptic," as she writes about her own changing perceptions. Again, this is informal writing, not meant to be graded—or necessarily ever read by someone else. But the journal writing assignment encourages her to explore and develop her ideas by forcing her still-liquid thought into concrete language.

Joan's final entry, a few days later, reflects on the value of this expressive assignment:

Before I hand this in, I have to write a short blurb on what I thought of this journal idea. I have to admit, at first I wasn't too fired up about it—I thought "what am I going to find to write about?" The first few entries were hard to write. But, as time went on I grew to enjoy it more and more. I actually found out some things about myself too. Anyway I did enjoy this and feel I like would be giving up a good friend if I quit writing in it!

The
End
(for now!)

Personal writing, in other words, can help students individualize and expand their learning by encouraging them to force the shadows in their mind—as Vygotsky says—into articulate thought. Art Young (1983), in studying both expressive and poetic writing, argues that such writing not only encourages students to learn about certain subjects and express themselves, but also that it gives them the time "to assess values in relation to the material they are studying." Certainly we witness our philosophy student using her journal to mediate between her personal values when she enrolled in class and the somewhat different ones presented by the professor during the course. The key, of course, is that the journal provides for the capture of these shifting, sometimes colliding, continually developing thoughts. Other academic documents dwell primarily on final, finished versions of thought and do not reveal the process by which these final thoughts were achieved.

READING AND EVALUATING STUDENT JOURNALS

Reading student journals keeps teachers in touch with student experiences—frustrations, anxieties, problems, joys, excitements. Teachers who understand the everyday realities—both mental and physical—of student life can be better teachers because they can tailor assignments and tests more precisely to student needs. In other words, reading student journals humanizes teachers.

Some teachers insist on not reading student journals, arguing they have no right to pry in these private academic documents. It is a good point. However, there are important reasons why the teacher ought to look at the journals—and precautions which can eliminate prying. First, for students just beginning to keep journals, a reading by a teacher can help them to expand their journals and make them more useful. Sometimes first journals have too many short entries; a teacher who notices this can suggest trying full-page exercises to allow writers more space to develop an idea. Second, some students believe that if an assignment isn't seen by a teacher, it has no worth. Thus, the teacher may decide at the outset that looking at the journals will add needed credibility to the assignment. Third, students feel that journals must "count for something," as must every requirement in a high school or college setting. And, "If teachers don't look at these things, how can they count 'em?"

One way to count a journal as part of the student's grade is to count pages. Some teachers grade according to the quantity of writing: 100 pages equals an 'A'; 75 a 'B'; 50 a 'C'; etc. Other teachers attempt to grade on the quality of insight or evidence of personal growth. Still other teachers prefer a credit/no credit arrangement: to complete the requirements for the course, students must show evidence that they have kept a journal. Teachers need only see that pages of journal writing exist; they don't need to read the entries. While fair, this method precludes the teacher from learning through students' writing.

To resolve this apparent paradox between the students' need for a private place to write and the benefit to both student and teacher from a public reading, I ask students to keep their journals in a looseleaf format and to provide cardboard dividers to separate sections of the journal. Thus, I am able to look at sections dealing with my course, but not to see sections more personal or concerned with other courses. And if portions of the student's commentary about a particular class would prove embarrassing, the looseleaf allows removal of that entry prior to my perusal. I may ask for the pages concerning American literature, for example, skim them quickly, and hand them back with suggestions only for those students who aren't gaining much from the experience. At the end of the course, I may check the journals again and assign a credit/no credit mark. Or I may raise student grades for good journals (lots of writing) but not penalize students for mediocre ones. Such informal evaluation doesn't take much time, but the benefits to both students and teacher are obvious.

Near the end of the term, I usually ask students to prepare their journals for a "public" reading, to delete any entries too personal to share, and then to add page numbers, a table of contents for major entries, and an introduction. Finally, students write an entry in which they formally evaluate their own journal: "Which entries make the greatest impact on you now? Which seem least worthwhile? What patterns do you find from entry to entry?" For some students, this proves to be the clarifying activity of the term, the action which finally defines the journals. In other words, students use their journals to reflect on the value of journals. For many, this informal, non-graded writing is a new and pleasant experience. In the words of one student:

> The journal to me has been like a one-man debate, where I could write thoughts down and then later read them, this seemed to help clarify many of my ideas. To be honest there is probably fifty percent of the journal that is nothing but B.S. and ramblings to fulfill assignments, but, that still leaves fifty percent that I think is of importance. The journal is also a time capsule. I want to put it away and not look at it for ten or twenty years and let it recall for me this period of my life. In the journal are many other things besides the writings, such as drawings and pages from this years calendar. It is like a picture of this period of my life. When I continue writing a journal it will be of another portion of my life.
>
> [KEN M.]

TEACHER JOURNALS

Teachers who have not done so should try keeping a journal along with their students. Journals don't work for everyone; however, the experience of keeping one may be the only way to find out. Teachers, especially, can profit from the regular introspection and self-examination forced by the process of journal writing. The journal allows sequential planning within the context of a course. Its pages become a record of what has worked, what hasn't, and suggestions for what might work next time. Teachers can use journals for lesson plans, to work out practice exercises, and to conduct an on-going class evaluation. The journal may become a teaching workshop and a catalyst to generate new research ideas as well as a record of pedagogical growth.

Teachers should consider writing daily, in class, along with their students. Teachers who write with their students and read entries aloud lend credibility to the assignments. Doing the writing also tests the validity of the writing task; if the instructor has a hard time with a given topic, it provides an insight into the difficulties students may encounter and so makes for a better assignment next time.

The journal provides an easy means to evaluate each class session; the journal is not the only way to do this, of course, but it proves a handy place to keep these records, alongside the planning sessions and the in-class journal writes. One of my own entries, for example, written 10 minutes after class, reads like this:

> Class went well today—but much slower than I expected. I worked on "paper topics" with people—first privately in their journals, next in small groups, finally on the blackboard for the whole class to talk about. All were too broad and general—so I asked people to rewrite and redefine and refocus—in fact, I badgered people out loud to limit their topics. Badgered too much?

Jottings like this may help teachers understand better their own teaching process and sometimes result in useful insights about what should or shouldn't have been done. These evaluations also act as prefaces for the next planning session, pointing toward more structure or less. And when a class, for one reason or another, has been a complete failure, writing about it can be therapeutic; I try, at least, to objectify what went wrong and so create the illusion of being able to control it the next time.

Journals are interdisciplinary and developmental by nature; it would be hard for writers who use them regularly and seriously not to witness growth. Journals belong at the heart of any writing-across-the-curriculum program. They promote self-examination on the one hand and speculation about ideas on the other; as such, they are as valuable to teachers in the hard sciences as to those in the humanities. To be effective, however, journal use in one class should be reinforced by similar use in another class. Of course, for teachers in some disciplines the personal nature of journals may be of secondary importance, with the primary focus remaining the student's grasp of specialized knowledge. However, the importance of coupling personal with academic learning should not be over-looked; self-knowledge provides the motivation for whatever other knowledge an individual learns and absorbs. Without an under-standing of who we are, we are not likely to understand fully why we study biology rather than forestry, literature rather than phi-losophy. In the end, all knowledge *is* related; the journal helps clarify the relationships.

WORKSHOP ACTIVITIES

Pre-Chapter Journal Writing

Write for five minutes about one of the following topics:

1. What are your prior associations with journals? Do you keep one? Have you ever kept one? Do you know someone who has or does? Have you ever assigned one to students? With what results?
2. Can you imagine any reasons why students might benefit from keeping a journal in your subject area?
3. What problems have you had—or would you anticipate—when students keep journals in school?

Post-Chapter Journal Writing

Use your own journal to develop a plan for assigning journals in one of your own courses:

1. Which class that you currently teach would lend itself to journal assignments? Why do you think so?
2. Can you think of five specific journal assignments to ask your students to write during the first week of class next term?
3. What objections to assigning journals do you anticipate from colleagues? How might you answer them?

Workshop Exercise

Double-Entry Journal

One idea suggested by Ann Berthoff (1978) requires students to write regular entries on the right-hand notebook page and leave the left-hand page blank so the writer may add further thoughts about modifications of the ideas written on the right-hand page.

To explore this idea in one of your classes which is already keeping journals, start each Monday (or Tuesday) by asking students to return to one entry written the previous week (or weeks) and write their thoughts about the earlier thoughts. (10 minutes)

Ask for volunteers to read their revised entries aloud, including the original entry if necessary.

Repeat regularly in subsequent classes or make this a homework requirement for the remainder of the course.

Classroom Handout

Suggestions for Using Academic Journals

What Is a Journal?   A journal is a place to practice writing and thinking. It differs from a diary in that it should not be merely a personal recording of the day's events. It differs from your class notebook in that it should not be merely an objective recording of academic data. Think of your journal rather as a personal record of your educational experience, including this class, other classes, and your current extracurricular life.

What to Write.   Use your journal to record personal reactions to class, students, teachers. Make notes to yourself about ideas, theories, concepts, problems. Record your thoughts, feelings, moods, experiences. Use your journal to argue with the ideas and readings in the course and to argue with me, express confusion, and explore possible approaches to problems in the course.

When to Write.   Try to write in your journal at least three or four times a week (aside from your classroom entries). It is important to develop the *habit* of using your journal even when you are not in an academic environment. Good ideas, questions, etc., don't always wait for convenient times for you to record them.

How to Write.   You should write however you feel like writing. The point is to think on paper without worrying about the mechanics of writing. The quantity you write is as important as the quality. Use language that expresses your personal voice—language that comes natural to you.

Suggestions

1. Choose a notebook you are comfortable with; I recommend a small (6″ × 9″) looseleaf.
2. Date each entry; include time of day.
3. Write long entries; develop your thoughts as fully as possible.
4. Use a pen (pencils smear).
5. Use a new page for each new entry.
6. Include both "academic" and "personal" entries; mix or separate as you like.

Interaction. I'll ask to see your journal several times during the term: I'll read selected entries and, upon occasion, argue with you or comment on your comments. None of the dialogue with you will affect how much your journal is "worth." A *good* journal will be full of lots of long entries and reflect active, regular use.

Conclusion. At the end of the term please (1) put page numbers in your journal, (2) make a table of contents for significant entries, (3) write an introduction to the journal, and (4) an evaluation of its worth to you.

Teachers and Students Respond

Keeping Journals

1. The journal is useful to me because it forces me to think and forces out thoughts that otherwise might not come out. It disciplines the mind. It gets me thinking early in the morning. It forces me to appreciate the fact that listening and reading are active enterprises and that unless one reflects upon what one has heard and read it will not become part of one. I am reminded of a paradox. Homer, Socrates, and Milton (after his blindness) did not write; yet all three were brilliant thinkers. The key to understanding their brilliance is that they reflected on what they heard and read and what they thought. Writing a journal is not a substitute for thought or thinking itself; it is a tool that is useful in stimulating thought. Great minds can think without writing.

2.   This term was the first term that I did not find writing in a journal to be a tedious and hard process. I think one reason for this is that you never specified the number of journal entries we were required to write per week. I had the freedom to choose what and when I wanted to write.

I found the journal very helpful in analyzing pieces of writing. It seems that whenever I had read something now I must have a piece of paper handy to make notes and write questions. I find myself doing this for readings in my other classes so I must say that this journal has helped improve my study habits.

My journal entries were also helpful/useful when it came to writing my papers because I had written down some notes and ideas while the story was fresh in my mind and I could take these ideas and further develop them.

Finally, I found the journal helpful in my personal life. Like when I had trouble with a story. I would try to work out my personal problems on paper. All those journals have been destroyed by my choice, though.

I think I will probably continue to keep a journal from now on. It will probably be more on a personal level than "scholarly" level because I use my class notebooks for that type of writing. I would almost feel lost without having a journal around in which I know I could write when I wanted to put my thoughts down on paper.

3.   When I made up my table of contents I was forced to go back and reread practically all of my entries. For this entire term I was convinced I had no ideas of value in the journal. I repeated this belief in class several times. But now I find this isn't the truth. I was surprised to see how little I wrote about the dorm and my family and how many times I led up to full fledged ideas. They often were not fully developed. My entries served as jumping off points.

Before the Table of Contents I was unhappy with this journal. Now I am satisfied and can say it is finished.

3

Composing

Most of us who teach also write. We are writers, some better than others, but writers just the same. We have written through a dozen years of public or private schooling, have used writing to earn one or more college degrees, and have used written language in a variety of modes to further our personal and professional lives. While few of us think that writing is easy, most of us know we can do it when we need to. We know how to start and we know that starting is usually the hardest, messiest part. We know about how many times we need to run to the refrigerator or to the coffee pot during some long evening of composing. And we know where we can get help when we need it, who we can trust to find holes in our arguments or typos in our sentences. Experience has taught us about our own idiosyncratic way of putting words together on paper so that they make sense. Most of our students, however, have simply not had that much experience with writing to trust that either they can do it well or that learning to do it well is important.

We could help our students quite a bit if we shared some of what we know about writing—not what we know as "experts," but simply what we know because we are adults who accept writing as a useful and necessary skill in a literate culture. We need to show them that competent writing is both important and learnable—and often frustrating, messy, unpredictable, exciting, and joyful as well. The biggest difference between the frustrating, messy, etc. process of the professional and the novice is that the former *knows* the process is frustrating, messy, etc., but is not alarmed by it, while the latter does not and is. The professional *knows* that he or she can start a piece of writing one place and end up another and find a use for both; the novice does not. And the professional *knows* that, in the end, the process will work, will deliver some acceptable version of the required product; the novice does not. These are the things we must teach, as we ask our students to compose and as we respond to their composing.

LEARNING TO COMPOSE

If asked to outline more succinctly the phases through which
many pieces of writing pass on the way from conception to com-
pletion, I might suggest about five more or less distinct phases or
stages, acknowledging that this is but one version of many possible
and that furthermore this is an overly-tidy way of describing an
idiosyncratic process. Looking at this outline may, however, give
us some idea of how and where to start talking to our students
about their own writing. Here's such an outline:

1. Starting.
2. Searching.
3. Composing.
4. Revising.
5. Editing.

In going through each of these phases, experienced writers have
learned to ask certain questions—implicitly or explicitly—to move
the writing along.

In "starting" a piece of writing, they ask about what they
want to say and to whom to create what effect. They allow time
for ideas to run loose in their head as well as on paper. Writers
learn to trust certain techniques to get them going when ideas
aren't flowing—for example, making lists, diagrams, sketches, or
journal entries. Starting a piece of writing can include the dialecti-
cal insights gained in conversation as easily as a sequence of thought
generated while jogging two miles on a country road. Starting for
me includes knowing that certain rituals work one time, but not
every time. It also means *knowing* that whatever I start I will
finish if it's important enough.

"Searching" is easy to think about, difficult to begin and impossible to complete. You can always find something else or extra,
no matter how finished you feel or want to feel. Searching is an
exciting, many-faceted process—something every writer does to
write well. While libraries are the foundations of so much knowledge and decision-making that it is impossible to mention searching without thinking of library research, searching also happens in
dozens of less formal and organized ways: looking through magazines on the coffee table, remembering an article begun in the
dentist's office, asking a friend for an idea, interviewing an expert
for testimony, posing a problem to a class, reading old diaries, remembering where you've been and what you've seen and to whom
you've talked, to what conclusions you've come.

"Composing" is even harder than starting or searching. Composing implies producing sentences, paragraphs and pages in some

reasonable sequence; it is the stuff of discipline and duration. Composing also implies reading and rereading your draft constantly, as it develops, to see where you've been and where you're going.

"Revising" is the longest part of the process. It involves rereading and rethinking what you've said to see if you said what you meant to say or whether something else emerged. Revising differs from editing in that it suggests larger changes in the text—in paragraphs and whole pages. It implies certain procedures and tools: it depends on having double-spaced copy—whether typed, handwritten, or displayed on a word processor monitor. My tools are pencils, scissors, and stapler. I like to rearrange pages as I rethink them, cutting a page in half here, stapling it in place somewhere else, drawing arrows to connect this to that, calling a new run of pages 14A, 14B, 14C, 14D—rather than renumbering the whole batch then and there. Revising is when I discover what's missing and whether I need to go find it or to forget it.

Editing is most enjoyable. At this point in a piece of writing, I know where I've gone, at least for a few paragraphs or pages, if not the whole piece, and am reasonably sure that it holds together. Editing amounts to perfecting the particulars, cutting things out, deleting words and phrases that don't carry their weight in a given sentence, nor add information nor serve any rhetorical purpose. Editing also means finding repeated words—like "process" in this chapter—and replacing them with synonyms. It means combining some sentences, condensing others, and recasting still others. And editing means finally looking up those words I'm not sure how to spell and getting them right once and for all—not to mention catching awkward grammar, missing punctuation, and sexist pronouns. The last stage of editing, in other words, is proofreading, where tinkering must stop and typos be caught.

This five-part schema is neither unique nor universal; it does represent, however, a general—if simplified—process which can be encouraged and taught by most teachers in most disciplines with generally positive results. Assignments can be made and evaluated in accordance with this process, and writers who learn to trust the process will create an ultimately reliable system.

TEACHING A PROCESS APPROACH TO WRITING

Knowledge of the writing process can influence a teacher's pedagogy in two distinct, yet related ways. First, the teacher who studies the various activities which are necessary to accomplish a given writing assignment may make use of that knowledge in assigning and evaluating writing in his or her course. For example, such a teacher is more likely to ask for writing in several draft stages and to respond differently to each draft, depending upon what strengths or weaknesses the piece of writing reveals. Teaching this way helps students to see writing as involving various actions which take place over time and shows them how to gain some control over the actions.

The second influence of the writing process upon pedagogy stems from the relationship between writing and learning. The teacher who asks students to start a writing assignment by making informal journal entries first soon discovers that they help students clarify any information—and hence adopts journal writing as a component in the course, independent of formal writing assignments. Yet another example comes from a later stage in the process, where a teacher discovers that editing skills which students use to sharpen academic prose are similar to the close reading skills needed to critically decipher turgid textbook prose; this teacher regularly asks his students to rewrite textbook prose into their own words to facilitate their understanding of difficult ideas. The point in both examples is that writing increases the writer's understanding, in addition to whatever communication function it also serves, and so is useful in any discipline and at every grade level.

Most teachers depend on writing to serve an evaluative function. Students are asked to write term papers, laboratory reports, essay exams, and expository prose of all sorts and are graded on how well these written products reveal students' knowledge or understanding. The teacher who examines what happens during the whole process, in addition to what is demonstrated by the final product, learns where students are having problems and where and what kind of help they need.

Whether or not they're aware of it, students do use a composing process in one form or another every time a teacher gives a writing assignment. Teachers who recognize this can make their students more conscious of how they compose and also use this knowledge in making, intervening in, and evaluating writing assignments. Consider again the five phases of a typical writing task and see what kind of help teachers might offer students in order to help them write better and value it more:

Starting

Finding a place to start poses problems. Experienced writers have tricks or techniques to get started, whereas novices don't. Teachers can help by carefully introducing each writing assignment. Consider the following suggestions:

1. Find out in advance how much students know and don't know about the kind of writing you are asking for. Do they know what a research paper is and know it differs from a book report or personal opinion paper? You can discuss these differences before they begin to write.
2. Try to stimulate personal involvement between writer and writing assignment. This can be done not only by giving a variety of choices in topics, but also by engaging students in dialogues about potential topics and asking them to keep journals (and therefore dialogues with themselves) about what is and isn't important to them.
3. Create class contexts for writing assignments. This may be obvious, but a few suggestions might be in order: bring in outside speakers on the topic, take context-producing field trips, assign and discuss relevant readings, and engage in clarifying class discussion.
4. Pose problems to the class, or ask the class to pose problems. Use the blackboard or overhead projector liberally so that problems in need of written solution are visually clear and precise. Demonstrating how "issue trees" or flow charts help clarify problems may help. Ask students to consider papers as solutions to these problems (or answers to posed questions); this approach makes it easier for students to understand what a thesis is and what they need to prove.
5. Lead up to assignments with deliberate invention techniques, including oral brainstorming, freewriting and journal writing. Most of us who have graduated from college have learned, often the hard way, to write notes to ourselves, to outline and to talk with others to get our writing started in the right direction; we can teach our students to use these techniques to start most writing assignments.

Searching

As we have seen, searching can involve a wide variety of activities, in addition to library use. Experienced writers have been rewarded by their searching efforts and have learned that discipline, perseverance, and inventiveness pay dividends. Novice writers have not found this out. Consider the following suggestions:

1. Pose real problems, or problems that exist in the student's own environment. The extent to which a class assignment touches a writer's own academic or personal experience is the measure of how much information can be found or searched for in his or her immediate environment.

2. Ask students to locate some of their information by interviewing local people. Interview techniques can be discussed in class and this real-life way of collecting information often creates much deeper involvement in the topic because information so gathered is actually "new" or "created" information, not arising from books or other people's searching.
3. Ask colleagues to assist your students in finding information. Such collaboration reflects the way people work in business and industrial settings, and creates helping networks among both faculty and students within the school setting. Information gained by consulting experts directly is alive and current; students learn to value that.
4. Spend a couple of class periods in the library with your students. Make it clear that you are there to help—as are the librarians. This is especially helpful for students who have never frequented the library.
5. Show the class the fruits of some of your own searching efforts. Use an opaque or overhead projector and show students how a piece of your writing has developed because you searched well. Students enjoy seeing your work as much to learn more about you, their teacher, as to see how a concrete, professional job of searching is done.

Composing

At some point writers need to start a draft. Composing it is one of writing's major hurdles. Some students believe they must follow rules, must get a thesis sentence first, must begin with an outline. Teachers can put such rules in another context by offering these suggestions:

1. Plan to throw the first page away. Writers who tell themselves this reduce the tension connected with actually starting a draft. Whether or not the page is thrown away doesn't really matter. The advice gets words on a page—and may even lead to articulating the thesis statement in the process.
2. Teach that writing shapes thesis. For most writers, thinking versus writing is a constant process of negotiating. Think about your thesis, yes, but also write about it as a means of thinking about it. Try one formulation, then another, in words, and evaluate and modify that until you're satisfied.
3. Suggest that student writers list five possible theses—and then list the opposite of these five. Or do the same with titles. This allows the writers to see how sharp and clear any one thesis is. It is a good class exercise, both at the beginning of a writing assignment and after students have begun to write.

4. Talk briefly about outlining, giving several models. Most have learned the standard I, A, 1, a, model (where there's a 1 you are morally obliged to have a 2); point out that outlines simply structure direction and purpose, and that key words or phrases jotted on scrap paper serve well as outlines.
5. Let the writing shape the outline. Many professional writers outline only *after* they have written a good portion of a draft. Let the process work here; once writers have seen the direction mind and pen are taking, they can stop and see what kind of outline makes sense. Any piece of writing can be structured in a variety of ways; deferring the making of an outline sometimes gives the writer more choices and options.

Revising

This activity obviously takes place all the time in a serious piece of writing. Thus, revising shouldn't be perceived as a cut-and-dried, one-step practice. The mental process that generates revision (re-vision, re-viewing, re-reading, re-thinking) can be worked with, and there are certain techniques and strategies for teaching it. More on this in a later chapter; for now, consider the following suggestions:

1. Assign papers in multiple-draft stages: draft one due third week; draft two due fifth week; final draft due seventh week. This allows you to intervene in the process through written comment and conference to help student writers sharpen their writing—and their thinking.
2. Focus your comments to students on particular problems at particular draft stages. For example, if the student writer is having trouble "over-generalizing," because he has no detail or support for his position, comment on that and don't worry about his style, documentation, or lack of subheads. Work hard and positively on that single issue, and almost certainly the writer will learn better how to support an argument for the next time.
3. Use peer revision groups in class. One exercise particularly effective when the first draft is due is to (a) collect the papers, (b) divide the class into groups of three to five, (c) hand back the papers to be read round robin in groups, with comments made in pencil, and (d) conclude by returning papers to owners and allowing students to hand in or *revise* and hand in next time.
4. Bring to class an anonymous sample short paper written by a student the year before. Distribute copies and ask small groups to examine it for possible revision. Students see problems in

others' writing before they learn to see those same problems in their own. You can select a paper which has a particular problem—lack of support, for example—and ask the students to focus particularly on that issue. (In this exercise, you'll find the wisdom of the group to be greater than any one individual's, which will usually result in first-rate revision suggestions. You'll also find that good suggestions will vary markedly, which will show students that the revision process encourages options, not right answers.)

5. Show samples of your own writing in several drafts on an opaque or overhead projector. Let students see (a) that serious revision is more than a shuffling around of a few commas, (b) that revision is messy, and (c) that your thinking is not elegant the first time either.

Editing

This activity, like revising, goes on all the time and doesn't take place in one neat stage of writing. Nor is editing as sharply distinct from revising as I'm suggesting. Nevertheless, to demonstrate editing as a discrete activity has certain advantages. Here students can learn to pay particular attention to sentence-level problems. Try these activities to work on a variety of problems, from style to mechanical correctness:

1. One way to teach students to write good sentences is to ask them to practice rewriting their own sentences, over and over, to achieve a variety of effects. To do this the first time, take 15 minutes at the end of a class and (a) ask students to write one sentence to sum up what they learned in class today, (b) rewrite that same sentence three different ways, and (c) exchange sentences with another student and suggest three more rewrites to each other.

2. Divide students into editing pairs before written assignments are due; require that students read and edit each other's papers before they are handed in. If you like, grade both the editor and the writer. Should certain pairs be particularly successful, keep them for the whole term. Such collaboration asks each student to practice both writing and critical reading skills—both essential components of the editing process.

3. Create editing review sheets which identify particular problems for students to work with. Problems to identify: repetition, generality, vague words, wordiness, incorrect punctuation, spelling, grammatical agreement, etc. (See sample critique sheet in Chapter 6.) Such activity can be done outside

of class, yet students have the benefit of your guidelines to point them in certain directions. Ask that such sheets be appended to written assignments, and review these to see how accurately students can diagnose their own writing.

4. Pass out a short sample student paper that exhibits certain editing problems—wordiness, for example—and ask students to edit, first individually, then in groups of three. Request that groups agree on a consensus editing—the "best" from three versions. This exercise can be done in 30 minutes, once a term, with discipline-relevant materials, and will provide useful guidelines for the remainder of the term.

5. Misspelling is the most obvious flaw in many student papers because it is easiest to identify by literate readers (you). However, it is generally a minor problem in terms of the quality of ideas in a given paper. If you use a process approach, it is best to reserve comments on poor spelling for later drafts—to point out early that there are some spelling problems that the student must attend to before a final draft is turned in, but that right now you want to help the student work on his or her organization or thesis or the quality of documentation. A process approach attempts to put spelling in its place, whereas a product approach may overemphasize spelling at the expense of more major concerns.

The problems discussed above were mentioned by teachers committed to helping students write better. Many of the suggestions for solutions grew directly out of discussions with teachers in disciplines other than English. There are dozens of other solutions for starting, composing, etc. not addressed here. (See Chapter 9.) These suggestions have worked for some instructors in some situations. Their importance results from the process approach which generated them; they are, consequently, compatible. Teachers who experiment with these suggestions will find that some work and some don't; some fit naturally into the way they teach a course, while some would radically alter course structure and teacher pedagogy. Accept these suggestions in the smorgasbord style in which they are offered, and you will create your own useful system.

A final thought: the problem of students who are afraid to write. Teachers who use a process approach to making written assignments will, at the same time, reduce student anxiety about writing. Much of the frustration that develops into fear stems from the unrealistic, unsympathetic, and unconsidered demands often made by teachers. A process approach to writing recognizes the complex and difficult nature of the composition process and frames each assignment in a context that develops explicitly from course material. Writing approached in a process manner becomes a more friendly and familiar activity because writers are allowed to negotiate their way more reasonably as they move through it. Writing resumes its natural place at the center of intellectual inquiry and exposition and becomes the clarifying companion to all the other learning activities—reading, speaking, computing, viewing, and listening. Writing is an essential activity to create order from chaos, sense from nonsense, meaning from confusion; as such it is the heart of creative learning in both the arts and sciences.

WORKSHOP ACTIVITIES

Pre-Chapter Journal Writing

Try a freewrite this time instead of a normal journal entry (Elbow, 1973). Write for 10 minutes in response to one of the following questions. Start writing about one topic as fast as you can, not stopping to stare at the ceiling, reread, revise, edit, or think. As you will see if you have not written this way before, these "rules" which restrict how you can write also liberate you to put down thoughts or memories you might normally not. These may be useful in themselves or useful in bringing out still more things once known and now forgotten or misplaced in some deep recess of our mind.

1. How, when, and where did you learn to write? (Start with the earliest memory at hand and see if the writing brings out others.)
2. How do you write? (Think here about the process you use to actually compose a fairly serious piece of writing.)
3. What was the most difficult writing you ever did? What circumstances made it so?

Post-Chapter Journal Writing

At your leisure, write about one of the following ideas:

1. Select one of the suggestions presented in this chapter and expand on it with your own teaching circumstances in mind.
2. Redesign one writing assignment which you currently give to your students in order to make them more aware of their own writing process.

Workshop Exercise

Composing (60 minutes)

To help students begin a piece of writing that will be due at a later date, try the following in-class sequence:

1. *Freewrite for 10 minutes on your paper topic. (10 minutes)
2. Read your own freewrite to a neighbor; tell him or her what your tentative thesis is; reverse roles. (5)
3. Freewrite again, focusing especially on the thesis you just articulated. (10)
4. Divide into groups of three and read either your first or second freewrite twice to your group. Listeners in the group should respond to the reading in one of two ways only:
   (a) Where did you want more information?
   (b) What struck you as interesting?
   The reader should not answer, but take notes. Repeat until each student has read and been responded to. (20)
5. Write in your journal how you felt doing any part of this exercise; share reactions if time.

Classroom Handout

Writing as a Process

Category	*Actions* *
I. Starting	Lists, diagrams, and doodles.
	Journal writing.
	Talking with people.
	Incubating on the run and in the tub.
	Freewriting.
II. Searching	Interviewing and asking.
	Getting into the library.
	Observing and finding.
	Remembering.

*Freewriting is a technique of free-association writing meant to get words on paper as rapidly as possible before the writer has time to edit or censor them. After freewriting, the writer may decide to edit or throw the whole thing away. When students freewrite in class, it's important that they have the right to keep private what they have written. Directions: Write fast, don't stop to reread, edit, correct, crossout, stare at the ceiling, or think. Usually one freewrites for a limited period of time; five or ten minutes is a long time. The best discussion of this technique is by Peter Elbow (1973).

III. Composing	With pencils or word processors. Connecting and focusing. Imagining your reader. Throwing away your first page.
IV. Revising	Rereading and rethinking. Developing and supporting. Asking for feedback. Using scissors, staples, and insert keys.
V. Editing	Clarifying and sharpening. Combining, condensing, and delete keys. Proofreading: spelling, punctuation, documentation, and grammar.

Teachers Respond

How Did You Feel Reading Your Freewrite to a Colleague?

1.   1. Reading, listing topics, choosing a topic! excited!
    2. Writing—frustrated. Answering it would be impossible to explain a thought this abstract in a 10-min. writing.
    3. Listening to and critiquing others' writing: awkward—too much difference between what they'd written and what I could suggest/respond.
    4. Reading my own: embarrassed! I knew perfectly well how obscure it was; I knew, too, what a good (impressive!) idea it was—the embarrassment of mixed pride and chagrin: I knew what a good thought this is and they can't know because I haven't been given the time to demonstrate it with enough concrete detail. Always a problem with my writing (and *living* for that matter)—my internal dialogue is clear enough, but I have trouble gauging how much *others* need to hear in order to understand: how much can I take for granted?

2.   It gave me a chance to make a point—or prejudice—about evidence.
    Also showed what I already know about myself, that I'm better at rewriting than on first draft. I was very impressed at how smooth and to the point both Tom's and Ken's efforts were compared to mine.

---

*Writing is not a fixed linear process; each action can occur any time and many times while you write.

I did not feel diffident about presenting my efforts, but I might have if I were a student. After all, I've been doing this for a long time.

This technique might work very well in seminars and small classes.

3. —Interesting to write without stopping—I've never done this before; I've always labored over every sentence and also surprised at the relatively lucid outcome despite the non-stop method.

—Definitely felt pressured in writing and "on exhibit" and exposed when forced to share contents with two other people. Some disappointment that my essay had not engendered lots of desire for listeners to seek more information—maybe it was boring? Maybe it was incomplete?

—Many feelings of "If only I had . . . (the time, the quiet, the right word, etc.)"—many excuses why it wouldn't be "great."

4

Writing for Readers

Writing is usually directed to someone for a reason. Sometimes to a friend, often a stranger. Every time we write to someone, we change our voice, if ever so slightly, as we select words, phrases, and formats most likely to convey our intent best. We do this even when we write to ourselves, in diaries and journals, for most of us maintain an image of ourselves and write both from and to that image. We don't always make sharp, conscious decisions about our language when we shape it toward someone else; more often as we compose we make quick, subconscious language choices and would be at a loss to explain, immediately after composing, each choice logically or consciously—though good reasons may be close at hand. Our sense of audience is inextricably involved in nearly every act of revision and editing that we do as we compose, and thus audience awareness deserves separate attention.

In the classroom, students commonly write to one audience: the teacher. Period. Furthermore, most students write to teachers for one reason: to be graded. Yet such school writing does little to give students either coaching or practice, because the limits of the communication situation are so carefully and artificially circumscribed. Furthermore, students are seldom given an opportunity to explore their first and best audience, themselves. Regardless of whom a piece of writing is ultimately intended for, the writer must first be pleased with it, feeling that it puts together well the combination of thought and expression to accomplish this or that purpose. As Bob Boynton, my editor, observes, "Our first audience is always ourselves. We must think our own writing good."

GOOD WRITING

The definition of "good writing" depends upon why we want to write to whom. For mature writers, experience, practice, and wisdom dictate form, style, and voice. For immature writers, each new writing situation is more experimental, risky, unpredictable and, hence, uncontrollable. Does this mean that only wisdom born of age will help people write better? Not necessarily, although many of us have experienced older adults in freshman classes who do seem to write better simply *because they are older.* The returning veteran, the former housewife, the person who has worked for a while after graduating from high school—these people often do write better than the typical 18-year-old. But, while age may have something to do with better writing, it is not a solution useful to the young people in both high school and college who need to work on their writing now. Confident people who know what they want to say to whom will be good writers. People unsure of why they are writing won't be. Classroom teachers can provide students with at least some of the practice and experience that life otherwise provides by asking them to write for a wider variety of real purposes and real audiences than they may have hitherto been aware of.

CLASSROOM AUDIENCES

Communication is different from evaluation. When students write to be graded, they seldom try to communicate new information. In this sense, the primary audience for most student writing is not a real audience at all. An authentic writer-audience relationship begins with the writing having something to communicate to an audience that wants to learn or needs to know something. In schools, this situation is reversed. The teacher usually knows what the student is writing about to begin with and, furthermore, knows *more* about the subject than the writer does—which situation many teachers perceive as essential if they are going to evaluate the student's writing. The problem is, of course, that such writing is often the *only* writing assigned.

The teacher's superior knowledge precludes the student's writing out of any real concern for communicating or sharing knowledge with the teacher; instead the student knows that his or her paper will be examined—not simply read—and so anxiety increases as sincerity decreases. Such anxiety is ironic since teachers who already know what students are writing about should be the easiest audiences to write for; they are able to fill in missing information and connections that inexperienced writers sometimes omit (Applebee, 1981). It is their roles as evaluators, however, that make these potentially friendly audiences difficult to write for. In addition, the teacher's superior position puts the student in a subservient role, writing "up," which encourages that most common school writing voice, which seeks to please and impress the audience. Finally, and maybe causally, the teacher audience often ends up being no audience at all for the student writer. Perhaps because of the artificiality of the communication act, much student writing exhibits a kind of impersonal, cliché-ridden, generalized voice that implies no audience in particular. Such writing will be neither lively, expressive, nor meticulously succinct: it will not be good writing because nobody, neither teacher nor student, really cares about it.

There are other audiences in school settings for whom students can write, in addition to the teacher-as-examiner. Both James Britton (1975) and Arthur Applebee (1981) have conducted research on the extent to which teachers exploit potential school audiences; both have found that the audience I have been describing, the teacher-as-examiner, is the dominant one for student writers. Both describe other useful audiences such as the following:

1. The writer's self.
2. The teacher-learner in a dialogue situation.
3. A wider audience within the school setting.
4. A wider audience, unknown to the writer.

Teachers who are interested in creating a classroom environment in which students write to different people who really care about their writing may develop assignments which address one or several of these other audiences.

THE WRITER'S SELF

Students can be asked to write to themselves both to aid their learning and to promote more active classroom discussion. Teachers in the sciences and social sciences often avoid this kind of personal, expressive writing in the mistaken belief that it is suited only to English or humanities subjects; in reality, we know that many scientists, from J. Robert Oppenheimer and Albert Einstein to James Watson and Francis Crick, kept journals to document and explore their professional quests in personal terms. Personal writing can provide a necessary bridge between the teacher's ideas and the student's understanding, and, as such, is a natural kind of writing for all sorts of exploratory learning situations. I've written at length in this text about using journals and expressive writing; suffice it to say that the audience shift from teacher to self is a profound and legitimate classroom practice which encourages students to write frankly and at the same time promotes an ease and fluency in writing style that other audiences cannot approach.

A WIDER AUDIENCE

When you ask students to write to other students in your classroom, you encourage student-student dialogue. Writing to fellow students is distinctly different from simply talking: written communication demands a precision and clarity that oral communication does not. At the same time, when students write to each other, rather than to teachers, a certain pretension necessarily drops away. Students see pomp and puffery as readily as teachers do and are, perhaps, even more put off by it. What's the point, in writing to a classmate who cannot grade you, of pretending or impressing? When students write to each other, just as when we write to colleagues, the different relationship necessitates a different language, demands of the writer a usefully different perception of how language facilitates real communication. A corollary to group writing is peer-group reading, which means that students who write to each other also read each other's work. Most readers can identify problems in clarity and meaning more easily in another person's work than in their own. When students read and respond to (or critique) each other's writing, they learn at the same time to identify problems in style, punctuation, and evidence that may occur in their own writing. A wide variety of activities is possible; the value of this audience group will depend on how imaginatively and sincerely the teacher treats such assignments.

WRITER-READER RELATIONSHIP

James Britton (1975) describes the ability to write clearly for a wide, unknown audience as one of the most demanding forms of writing. There is some evidence, he suggests, that the ability to create this general writer-reader relationship is the mark of a fully mature writer. The writer is asked to imagine an audience unlikely ever to be seen; consequently, the writer must supply complete context, anticipate all possible questions, and follow conventions as carefully as possible. Students can write letters to editors, stories and reviews for local periodicals, reports to concerned corporate or government figures. The grading of such writing is clearly secondary to its ability to elicit informed responses from readers in nonacademic settings.

TEACHER-LEARNER DIALOGUE

Most writing which is assigned and evaluated by teachers asks students to *show* how much they learned rather than *explore* their learning. Such writing is product oriented; that is, it presents ideas

or information in finished form. Another kind of student writing
to the teacher, more common in the early grades (and in some
English classes), aims to share the process of learning and discovery
with the teachers and seeks *response* rather than *evaluation.* Teachers who commonly assign writing in stages and comment on—but
do not grade—each stage are acting more like partners in a developing dialogue rather than as judges of knowledge. Often writing
begun in an exploratory dialogical situation becomes, of institu-
tional necessity, "examined" at the last stage of the process. However, the examiner role in such cases is more informed and considerably less intimidating to the student, who now knows, because
they have had dialogue, the teacher's concerns and interests
better—and knows that the teacher *is* concerned and interested in
the piece bring worked on.

REVISING FOR THE READER

When teachers care about the results of student writing rather
than measuring the student's worth, school writing begins to be interesting. In such circumstances, teachers give open-ended assignments which challenge student writers, and students write in an
attempt to communicate ideas or information to a teacher who
doesn't already know all the answers. Ideally, such writing triggers
a dialogue between writer and reader similar to that which professional writers and editors share. Teachers allow for exploratory
drafts, and students use the multiple-draft process to make their
writing ever clearer and more careful. Revising for a specific
audience—readers who care—is often the catalyst which helps
student writers improve their writing. In the following pages, we'll
explore what happens when a young writer begins to shape a piece
carefully toward a specific, known audience. The following are two
drafts of a piece of student writing, the first aimed at a rather vague
teacher audience, the next revised to address a more carefully de-
fined audience of peers.

During the first week in a course in technical writing, which I
recently taught at Michigan Tech, I asked students to talk about
what made good technical writing. Students mentioned a number
of important factors that they remembered from their experience
of reading technical texts and writing reports in other departments:
clarity, economy, precision, effective diagrams, etc. After a brief
discussion, I asked them to examine periodicals, journals, or textbooks from their own respective disciplines and choose a sample of
writing which they considered "good"; then I asked them to write

a review to explain: "What makes it good technical writing?"
Finally, I asked them to append the article reviewed to their brief
report. Because the class was composed of students majoring in a
variety of engineering and scientific disciplines, I knew I wouldn't
be familiar with many of their sources, but I was curious to find
out what sorts of writing they identified as "good technical
writing." The following two paragraphs are taken from a three-
page report by Bob; they are fairly typical of the writing received
from many students on their first assignment:

[no title]

The article "Wind: A Power Source for Forklift Trucks,"
written by R. C. Weber and J. Seifert, is an excellent example
of technical writing. The clipping that is attached does not do
justice to the article as a whole. The main portion of the article contained various charts and graphs that helped to clarify
and simplify the concepts of wind power utilization.

The faults of the article are few. The one confusing part
for me was in the italicized introduction. The authors say
"wind as an energy source has been eclipsed by electricity
and gas." In the preceding sentence the authors were relating
back to the days when wind was used to drive mechanical
devices like pumps and flour mills before the days of our
modern power systems. The quote seems out of place in this
article because wind is being used in a way that is really unre-
lated to its past duties of driving machinery. The new duty of
wind will be to supplement existing power systems by charg-
ing systems as in this case or assisting in actual operations of
mechanical systems.

On the whole, this first paragraph isn't bad. It mentions some
pertinent facts, uses simple, direct language, and makes the writer's
introduction clear. (Never mind, at this point, about some awkward stylistic elements; right now we are concerned with whether
or not we clearly understand what the author is doing and why.)
For readers unfamiliar with his discipline, mechanical engineering,
there may be some problems of context and definition. The second paragraph, however, presents more immediate problems, as the
author jumps quickly into a critique which assumes the reader's
familiarity with the article and the subject matter of mechanical
engineering. In other words, Bob has assumed I know more about
his subject than I actually do.

To the next class period I brought an opaque projector and projected a number of student papers (with names covered) on a screen for class scrutiny. I asked if each paper was clear and understandable, and to what degree the authors had followed the principles of "good technical writing" in their own works. As you might expect, the students were quick to recognize problems in each paper. They critiqued the papers for vague terminology, poor explanations, wordy style, and flawed mechanics. As you might also expect, several students were angry with me for asking that standards of good technical writing be applied to their writing. They argued that they were writing for the teacher, and that *I* understood the context of the assignment because *I* had made it. Yes and no. While it was true that I understood the assignment, it wasn't true that I necessarily understood the material they presented because it was from an outside discipline.

At the end of class, we agreed that they would rewrite the reviews, this time for a carefully specified audience—"an educated lay person"—someone like me, who was literate, but who might not understand the technical terms of specific disciplines like mechanical engineering or even English. Bob's next draft looked like this—again the first two paragraphs only:

A Review of Technical Writing

Michigan Tech students never really take time to consider how much technical writing they read and write. Good technical writing is concise, factual, complete, and written for a specific audience in a formal language style. The article Wind: A Power Source for Forklift Trucks, written by R. C. Weber and J. Seifert for the January 1981 issue of *Mechanical Engineering* magazine, is an example of good technical writing. The attached clipping illustrates some basic elements of technical writing that will be discussed.

Formulas, percentages, graphs, and drawings give precise information and eliminate wordy explanations of ideas needed to understand the problems and assets of wind power. The clipping contains some formulas, but the main body contains graphs of wind velocity changes with different times of the day and seasons. The article discussed efficiencies of various power supplies by comparing percentages of operating costs. A drawing of the wind power equipment is included to allow the reader to see what they are reading about.

Probably we would all agree that this is a more lucid, carefully explained draft than the first. Bob now has a title to set up reader expectations. He has a lead to provide context for his audience as well as more careful definitions ("Good technical writing is concise, factual, complete . . .") and more complete facts ("written . . . for the January 1981 issue of *Mechanical Engineering* magazine"). In addition, he completes his first paragraph by explaining why he has attached an article to this report.

The second paragraph expands on the notion of the first, outlining generally what the article is about and suggesting why it is a good sample of technical writing. Bob highlights such features as "formulas, percentages, graphs and drawings [which] give precise information and eliminate wordy explanations." As a lay reader and a teacher, I was pleased with this revision because it provided a more carefully developed context as well as more precisely explained information. (Again, never mind that we could make some stylistic suggestions.)

Bob made these changes for a number of reasons: first, the class critique of student papers had a significant instructional impact, since he made changes in the specific areas the class criticized other papers for; i.e., few had titles, complete statements of context, facts, etc. *All* of the papers were better the second time because their authors were more self-conscious about technical components of good papers. Second, Bob's paper also improved because he was writing to a specific audience, educated, but not expert—and he had taken the time to imagine what such an audience needed to understand in his writing. In the second version, he makes no assumptions that the reader is already familiar with the article being reviewed. Finally, the paper improved because it was a second draft; very likely the original review had been written only once before being handed in. Bob's writing might have improved even without a class critique and a specified audience, simply because he now put it through a revision process.

Note: the critique exercise with the opaque projector occupied about 30 minutes of class time, about half of a normal class period; thus, teachers in subject-area classes (as distinct from writing classes) could employ a similar method with little time lost to course content. In fact, I would argue, an increased self-consciousness about their written expression in relation to the needs of the reader would, to some extent, enhance students' understanding of course material; the need to explain it well to an audience is a good clue to the writers about how well they understand the material themselves. In this sense, the need to be clear to an audience reinforces the need for the writer to be clear to himself.

In asking students to critique each other's papers, instructors are drawing on powerful pedagogical principles. Consider that students are asked to think for themselves and generate standards upon which to base a critique. The degree to which the instructor does not modify or feel a need to add to the list is the degree to which the students' collective knowledge and wisdom are reinforced and validated. Consider too that using samples of recent student writing for classroom discussion increases the interest—ups the ante, so to speak—as some students witness their own prose being discussed (and others anticipate that they will be next). Furthermore, as students and instructor make positive comments, writers learn what they have done right, what works for their critical audience as well as what doesn't.

Writers need to know how the public reacts to what they have written. This way, writers like Bob, trying to generate prose in the privacy of a dormitory room or library carrel, can better imagine reader questions. An exercise like this has dozens of permutations, depending on course topic, class size, time available, and the instructor's relationship with the class. The essentials to keep in mind, however, remain putting students in an active, responsible role in determining criteria for good writing and giving writers a second chance to review and reconceive the work, without being penalized for initial shortcomings.

How teachers handle subsequent papers also depends on individual circumstances. Some teachers do such an exercise once, early in the term, and thereafter demand that student writing meet second-draft standards. Other teachers form critique pairs or groups and ask that all papers be put through a review process—outside of class—prior to submission. Still other teachers continue the public critique session throughout the term, believing that time so spent contributes to, rather than subtracts from, time spent on course content.

It isn't the purpose of this chapter to suggest which possible audiences are appropriate to each academic discipline. However, the role of audience in making a writing assignment more real must be considered by *any teacher* who wants students to learn to write better. Students who are challenged to communicate real knowledge and serious concerns to a variety of audiences most closely approximate the kind of writing asked for in nonacademic settings. Imaginative teachers can, with a little effort, break out of the traditional judgmental role and generate more situations in which students must genuinely communicate to them, as readers, something of interest.

WORKSHOP ACTIVITIES

Pre-Chapter Journal Writing

Write briefly in response to the following questions:

1. For whom do you most commonly write?
2. How do you envision this audience when you write?
3. How do you think your students would answer this same question?

Post-Chapter Journal Writing

Select one of the following topics and write a brief response:

1. Review the most recent writing assignments you have given in your classes. To what extent do they help students identify you as an audience?
2. Design three writing assignments for a course you currently teach which specify audiences other than yourself.
3. Describe three roles from which students in one of your classes could write.

Classroom Handout

Reading an Audience

1. Why am I writing this?
2. For whom am I writing?
3. How much do I know about this person or persons? (Likes? Dislikes? Values?)
4. How much about my subject do he/she/they already know?
5. What about my subject will interest this audience?
6. What terms or concepts will be unfamiliar and need explaining?
7. What format would most effectively convey this information?
8. What image or impression of me am I trying to convey?
9. What does my audience expect from this paper?
10. What action do I want my readers(s) to take after reading this paper?

Teachers and Students Respond

A Number of Concerns

1.   Can you think of any way for students to write to different audiences in your courses?

The obvious would be to have the students write to each other. This would give them an opportunity to use the style that I typically receive for term papers. In a term paper for my class I would prefer a more formal style—one that would be acceptable for a publication. It might be interesting to ask the student to do an initial write-up for their peers, ask for feedback from them and then do a formal write-up (publication style) that I would get. This would force them to distinguish between the audiences and to do some editing/rewriting.

2.   Define clearly what product we expect by defining the criteria which we will use to evaluate.

Use the criteria to evaluate and write comments and suggestions as to how they could make their papers better.

Give more assignments so that they have a chance to practice.

Possibly give them the opportunity to rewrite after we have evaluated or possibly before final evaluation but after constructive criticism.

3.   Honest writing is writing that is done to voice one's true opinions. It is not the kind of writing that is done to hand in on an essay for a teacher in most cases.

When I look at a piece of writing I can not always tell if it is "B.S.ing" for the teacher or if it is really what the writer felt. Some people become very adept at just writing what they are told to, to fill pages and rarely write their true feelings.

When I write a paper I always know when I am doing honest writing; it seems to flow. On the other hand I kind of sit and think about what else can I put down.

5

Revising

Rewriting makes good writing and better thinking. I rewrite for two reasons: to make what I've written clearer and to find even stronger things to say. A few writers do most of their composing in their heads, first getting clear their outline, then their prose, sentence by sentence; once finished there's not much more to do. If you are this kind of writer, who doesn't need to revise "to get it right," remember that most people don't or can't write like that. For many of us, the writing process is continual rewriting—getting something down, then returning to it over and over to rethink and reshape. In fact, Donald Murray (1978), Pulitzer Prize-winning author and journalist, insists flatly, "Writing is rewriting."

Like most facets of composing, revising is neither neat, predictable nor rule-governed. There are times when I write well the first time through so that all I need to do is tinker with a draft, rewrite a few sentences, delete a few words, and add some subheads. Other times, however, the writing is so awful that I may simply begin the whole piece over again, tossing out every sentence and paragraph laboriously constructed the day before. But I'm still revising, since my first thrown-away draft cleared the way for new and better constructions. Sometimes we write down what we need to get rid of before we can discover what we want to keep. Sometimes, by seeing our thought take shape, we can say: "No, that's not what I meant at all," and so go on to what we do mean. Peter Elbow (1973) writes that most writing is founded on double binds: "you can't find the right words till you know exactly what you are saying, but you can't know exactly what you are saying till you find just the right words. The consequence is that you must start by writing the wrong meanings in the wrong words; but keep writing till you get to the right meanings in the right words. Only at the end will you know what you are saying" (p. 26).

Revision is reviewing, of course, reseeing the words we started
with and thereby evaluating them with a little more distance and
perspective than we had the first time through. Journalist William
Zinsser (1980) explains: "The writer must therefore constantly ask
himself: What am I trying to say? Surprisingly, often, he doesn't
know. Then he must *look* at what he has written and ask: Have I
said it? Is it clear to someone encountering the subject for the first
time? If it's not, it is because some fuzz has worked its way into
the machinery. The clear writer is a person clear-headed enough to
see this stuff for what it is: 'fuzz' " (p. 12, italics mine).

If serious writers view revision as the operational core of the
composing process, why don't our students view it that way? All
too often they seem to believe that revision means shuffling around
a few commas on the paper written last night before turning it in
for a grade. While this generalization does disservice to serious student writers, it holds true for many others who simply never learn
the incredible power of language for both developing and expressing thought.

An equally common problem which sometimes causes discord
among faculty members in different subject areas is the student
who writes fairly well in English classes, but turns in vague, sloppy,
uncrafted work in biology, home economics, and business. Here we
are as likely to be describing a sophomore in college as well as in
high school, both of whom are likely to view writing as a rather
perfunctory operation—busy work—which has no direct link to
either school learning or career success. For whatever reasons,
many students have grown up with little regard for the craft of
writing. Ironically, older students, who have made some effort to
return to school, often interrupting a career or in the midst of
raising a family, view writing as serious life-supporting work; they
have learned that literate people get good jobs and fast promotions
and perhaps even communicate better with friends and family. But
few of our college or high school students develop this seasoned
perspective and consequently they continue to treat writing instruction as more hurdle than help.

We who are English teachers *do know* some things about
teaching writing, but the lessons don't last because we can't teach
motivation. That needs to come from somewhere else. We need an
academic equivalent to the "employment imperative" which seems
to motivate older students, one that functions at the high school
or college level, to motivate students to become mature writers.
Such help can come most readily from colleagues who teach subjects other than English. Teachers in the student's major department are far closer to the student's prospective world of work than

English teachers are. Nor do chemistry, sociology or business teachers suffer from the same long-term stigma as English teachers who have too faithfully red-penciled misspelled words on student compositions all their professional lives—a breed obsessed about the minutiae of correctness.

The problem at many schools—high school and college alike—is the absence of a comprehensive literate environment to encourage, reinforce, and demand good language habits, including reading and speaking as well as writing. Without such an environment, there is little pressure on students to take writing seriously. Which is to say that if the lessons taught in writing classes are not reinforced in the student's other classes, those lessons won't be learned. While most teachers know, experientially and intuitively, that revision is necessary for good writing, these teachers seldom make writing assignments which reflect that tacit knowledge. Their understanding of writing has not been translated into classroom pedagogy. While a few teachers continue to insist that writing is strictly the business of English teachers, most teachers simply haven't thought much about teaching writing nor have some felt confident enough about their own writing to teach it to someone else.

REVISING FOR THE WRITER

Students revise their work, regularly, in every class I teach, whether it's a writing course, such as Technical Writing, or a content course, such as American Literature. I ask young writers to revise, obviously, because I want to help them to learn to *write* better; I also ask them to revise because I want them to *learn* better. As we discussed in Chapter 1, "Writing and Learning," seeing your language on paper lets you play with and develop that language. Much poor writing and thinking at both high school and college levels results from students who haven't yet learned to manipulate language on paper to better understand and develop it. While writing in the first place lets us see what we've got—what we know—*revising* what we've written really begins to tease it into sense. So we revise not only to communicate well with our audience, but to carry on a better dialogue with our own ideas.

To explain better what is meant by revision as a learning tool, let me show you some brief samples of a student writing; here, the first two paragraphs from a 13-page paper, then the first two paragraphs from the revised paper, which numbered eight pages. It would, of course, be more instructive to see the complete papers; however, these samples should illustrate my point.

This paper was written by Cathy D., a senior in a class on communications theory. As one of two major assignments in the course, I asked students to prepare a report on "The University as a Communications System." While the topic is broad, the context of the course readings (Orwell, Barthes, McLuhan, Freire, Ellul, Toffler), as well as class discussions, provide some direction to students about how to limit and focus the topic to make it manageable. Part of the process requires that students submit a proposal early in the term, have a first-draft conference with me at midterm, and turn in a preliminary draft three weeks prior to the final draft, for a thorough written critique to suggest final improvements. The paragraphs which follow were submitted as the preliminary draft, three weeks prior to the due date for final copy.

[Untitled]

Michigan Technological University's entire computer operations has been divided into eight separate divisions in an effort to organize groups into departments with common responsibilities and objectives. The entire organization is under the authority of . . . , the Director of University computing services. To assist him, the Vice President of Academic Affairs and the Vice President of Operations and Finance appoint a Computer Advisory Council. This council is composed of faculty and administrative members and is meant to be representative of the University and of computer users. Members of council are to help make decisions on or involving policies and procedures. They are also dispersed well enough throughout the services divisions and curriculums to act as a channel for matters and questions concerning computer Services. It is easy to find out who to contact in case of question, for the ACS library and Newsletter are readily available to those for direction.

The first specific branch discussed here is the most commonly known one, Academic Computing Services. This division makes use of a UNIVAC 1100 with 524K memory units. The computer is located in the Administration Building while the input-output devices and staff offices are located in the basement of the EERC Building. The computer machinery you see in the ME-EM Building is also a part of the UNIVAC, this remote batch station uses the main control unit in the Ad Building and is supervised through an electronic monitoring system by the student batch station operators in the EERC. The remote batch station has two "hot-lines" in case of any break down or questions. One line directly accesses the person in the Controlling unit in the Ad Building and the other contacts the present operator in the regular batch stations.

That Cathy's paper lacks a title may provide the best clue to the paper's focus: there is none. It begins by talking about the "University's entire computer operations" in the first sentence, yet provides no clues to reader (or writer?) about why this subject is introduced or what it has to do with a report on "The University [Michigan Tech] as a Communications System." The second paragraph is peppered with mysterious acronyms (UNIVAC, EERC, ME-EM) and numbers (1100, 524K), as well as such seemingly important matters as "remote batch stations" and "input-output devices." We're not fully certain what they are or why they're included.

Apparently, Cathy has collected numerous pieces of information to complete an assignment which she doesn't fully understand. (In her defense, the assignment is a difficult one, asking students to use their wits to put the report together; they must use interviews and site visits, for example, as much as any textbook or library, and synthesize a great deal of information to make a coherent report. An apologetic note accompanied the paper, indicating that Cathy knew she didn't have a handle on the assignment.) The paper continues in the vein suggested here for 12 more pages of unconnected, unfocused pieces of information rather than a complete report.

I wrote the following response to Cathy about her first draft:

> Your note to me suggests that you know where this is weak; number one job is to get a focus (why are you telling me this?) and organize your ideas to elaborate upon and explain that focus. I find a possibility on p. 6—maybe another on p. 8. But you need to determine what would be interesting and provocative to read. . . .
>
> First 5 pages go nowhere—just describe—I'd reduce that to a page or an appendix, and get on with *what makes* computers on campus a communications system—and what *about it*?
>
> A good bunch of information collected so far . . . work on focus plus integration. Can you make a "problem statement" from this? Find two sides to a debate here? Find a "tension" or "contradiction" to explain? Could Freire or Barthes or Orwell help?

Like many teacher comments, my response probably suffers from hasty composing, but I've tried here to raise the sort of questions which will provide a focus for the student's next draft. Cathy completely rewrote the paper as a result of these comments; following are the first two paragraphs of her final report:

Computer Services at Tech

A Brief Look at the Fastest Growing Communication Channel at MTU and the People Who Operate It.

To what extent do computers affect the academic, administrative and regular services at Michigan Technological University? Computer Science has become required in every technological field offered and is now essential to almost all technological study and graduate research. This comprises huge amounts of student processing, and yet, this takes up less than half of the University's computation workload. For the most part, students aren't the data processors, but the data being processed. This is easy to imagine when considering the vast amounts of scheduling and finance work done on computers alone. In this paper I will look at the breakdown of the all-university Computer Services, and look at the most predominant attitudes of those who deal with them. I will firstly focus on the people in authority over university policy, then the people employed by the University, and finally the students dealing with computers at MTU. I have found all the information available to me surprisingly interesting.

"If the auto industry had progressed as rapidly in capabilities and cost reduction as the computer industry has in the past 30 years, today a Rolls Royce would be on the market for $2.50 and would run on 2,000,000 miles per gallon." . . . , the director of MTU's all university Computer Services set the pace for our interview with this information. Imagine the impact of this on a school that has grown in size and technology as ours has. From a school where a slide rule was standard equipment for all students to one where there are more handheld calculators among the student body than students. It would be virtually impossible for Tech to even schedule one term without computers to process the minimum 30,000 drops and adds filled out.

These paragraphs reflect a direction born of confidence which the earlier fact-oriented writing completely lacked. While by no means perfect (she received a B on the finished paper), this draft does two things for the reader which the previous one failed to do: (1) it explains why the paper was being written ("To what extent do computers affect the academic, administrative and regular services at Michigan Technological University?"), and (2) it provides some interest and excitement to make the reader want to continue (e.g., the director's quote, the calculator statistics). The audience interest has picked up because the writer began to understand what she was doing with the report.

Cathy writes to answer my questions about focus; in the process, she writes her way into a better, more thorough understanding of the assignment. Had I simply graded the first paper turned in, she would not have kept learning. Had she done even more drafts, answering yet another series of questions, she would have learned even more about computers at Tech. Following is my final response to her:

> This report is much better; you have made it problem oriented, more integrated and more smoothly organized. The focus on computers remains consistent and the interviews are used well. You are less successful at integrating course texts which would provide an overview to put the computer system clearly at the heart of modern communications systems—where do you talk about what computers actually *do* in the communication process? The only evidence here seems to be that they screw up records. . . . And I miss the orientation that subheads could provide, miss physical description and some attempt to include extra data in a clearly organized Appendix.
>
> Overall the report is successful, which shows a lot of growth from earlier, less focused drafts. Minor errors mar this success to some extent, as do problems noted above. You do engage me in the concern over problems, which is a major plus for your prose style.

Again, my comment is neither profound nor a model of instructor prose style; rather it calls attention to the role of revision in learning. By commenting on the positive as well as the negative aspects of students' papers, by asking even more critical focusing questions and by withholding grades from these early, more exploratory drafts, instructors are able to help motivate students to both learn to learn and learn to write better.

IDEAS FOR REVISION

Here are some concrete ideas by expert writing teachers to help writers reshape their work. None works all the time nor for everyone, but one may help you out when your usual practice is not working.

Work with Paragraphs

Ann Berthoff (1978) makes a sharp distinction between "revision" on the one hand and "correcting" on the other: "When you revise, you compose paragraphs. You write sentences; you re-write paragraphs. It's only when you have several sentences—a paragraph in formation—that it makes sense to try to rewrite any one sentence." Berthoff suggests that writers work with paragraphs when they revise—not sentences—because only paragraphs provide enough *context* and *direction* to guide the revision. Writers who pause over every sentence soon get sidetracked, because they lose sight of their larger train of thought: "Concentrating on correctness while you're composing sentences would be like polishing the handle before the door is hung."

Don't Force It

Donald Murray has written more specifically about revising and composing for longer than anyone else I know. His essays on revising first reached me in 1967, the year I began teaching and his good sense has influenced me ever since. In the following excerpt, Murray (1980) describes what usually happens when people revise: "The final state in the writing process is *revising.* The writing stands apart from the writer, and the writer interacts with it, first to find out what the writing has to say, and then to help the writing say it clearly and gracefully. The writer moves from a broad survey of the text to line-by-line editing, all the time developing, cutting, and reordering. During this part of the process the writer must try not to force the writing to what the writer hoped the text would say, but instead try to help the writing say what it intends to say."

Share Your Writing

Ken Macrorie has waged war long and hard on "Engfish," the kind of writing which students think English teachers want, which has no honesty or personal commitment in it, which most English teachers want nothing to do with. To teach students to write more honestly, he teaches them to trust themselves and each other more. One of his favorite techniques is "the helping circle," literally a circle of people who take turns reading their own writing to each other and giving responses to each other. Macrorie (1976) writes:

"So the circle—at times frightening to every writer—is her third best resource. First, her own experience (including thoughts, feelings, and knowledge she picks up from others). Second, her skills as a writer. And third, the help the circle gives her to sharpen and hone those skills."

The help Macrorie refers to leads necessarily to revision: as each person reads his or her piece to the others, they in turn tell the writer what works for them, what doesn't, what else they might like to see, where to expand and add detail, etc. This way, writers help each other and revision becomes a natural part of each serious student's process.

Revise Whole Drafts

The late Mina Shaughnessy spent years studying the writing of "basic writers" in the open admissions program at the City University of New York. In addition to teaching the essentials of correct sentence grammar to these often disadvantaged students, Shaughnessy (1977) argues that they must be taught concurrently to write and revise whole compositions, as these are significantly "more gratifying" than writing sentence drills. She offers the following simple schema for introducing these inexperienced writers simultaneously to the demands of an audience and the need for form in writing:

Listener	*Writer's Response*
1. What's your point?	Thesis statement.
2. I don't quite get your meaning.	Restatement in different words.
3. Prove it to me.	Illustration, evidence, argument.
4. So what?	Conclusion.

Here, succinctly stated, are easy questions for peer readers to ask writers in order to generate significant revision.

Ask Questions

William Zinsser gives especially good advice to general readers based on his many years as author of books and journalist for the New York *Herald Tribune.* Zinsser (1980) describes the importance of asking basic questions about your writing at the very start and returning to these same questions over and over again as you re-read and revise: "In what capacity am I going to address the reader?" (Reporter? Provider of information? Average man or woman?) "What pronoun tense am I going to use?" "What style?" (Impersonal reportorial? Personal but formal? Personal and casual?) "What attitude am I going to take toward the material?" (Involved? Detached? Judgmental? Ironic? Amused?) "How much do I want to cover?" "What one point do I really want to make?"

While experienced journalists might be able to make rapid answers to these questions, student writers need to realize, first, that asking such questions implies conscious choice over material and, second, that they may need to re-ask these questions over and over again as they develop their material. The writer who can answer these questions quickly will gain control of his or her writing from the start.

In addition, Zinsser (1980) stresses the importance of writing as discovery, which process may lead the writer into new territory and force reconsideration of stance, style, or subject: "Don't fight such a current if it feels right. Trust your material if it is taking you into terrain that you didn't intend to enter but where the vibrations are good. . . . Don't ever become a prisoner of a preconceived plan." Essentially, Zinsser argues that an initial set of questions combined with a willingness to trust new currents of thought make confident writing: "scissors and paste are honorable writer's tools."

Write to Yourself

Linda Flower discusses revision primarily in rhetorical terms. She believes that many writers need a two-stage process, with first drafts written primarily for themselves (writer-based prose) and subsequent drafts aimed more and more consciously towards external readers (reader-based prose). Writers are most likely to write personal or expressive prose when they confront new or confusing material. Flower (1981) writes: "The more complex your problem and the more difficult your material, the more you will need to transform your writer-based prose to reader-based prose." Flower's point is that writing for oneself first is both helpful and natural; before writers can communicate to someone else, they need to understand the material fully themselves. And the act of writing leads to that of understanding. In this context, writers revise so that readers, too, may understand most clearly what writers have to say.

Write Freely

Peter Elbow advocates starting fast and letting the writing generate the thinking. He is perhaps best known for his lucid instructions on how to "freewrite," a rule-governed exercise that asks the writer to write for a fixed period of time as fast as possible without stopping to think or revise. A corollary to this kind of brainstorming on paper is, of course, revision. As Elbow (1981) writes: "If you haven't found your main point during the writing process, now you must demand it. This is often a crucial, delicate, frustrating process. You have lots of good stuff, but as you turn it over and over, you can't find the center, the main point, the one thing that sums it up. You are trying to wrestle a powerful snake into a bottle. It writhes and writhes and you can't get control over it. You have two main options, putting it aside and wrestling some more." My own method of revising tells me that Elbow is right: sometimes the best way to shape a piece better is to leave it alone for awhile and let your unconscious mind grapple with it in some subterranean way. Other times, nothing else will do than to work it out, right there, analyzing, dissecting, rewriting until the "center" emerges.

Look at Your Language

Janet Emig (1978) writes that "the eye is the major instrument by which we re-scan and review what we have written." Citing the example of Jean Paul Sartre, who quit writing when he became blind, she suggests that we teach our students the relationship between reading and rewriting. Revision does not happen in a vacuum—or inside the cerebral cortex when cut off from visual stimulation. Writers need to be methodical readers of their own work to recognize that re-vision is the key to revision.

Trust New Ideas

Nancy Sommers (1980) questioned the differences between the revision strategies of student writers and experienced adult writers. In her research she discovered that students more often sought to revise their writing to match a predefined meaning, to make their writing turn out as they expected it—or thought teachers wanted it to—from the start. By contrast, "experienced writers see their revision process as a recursive process—a process with significant recurring activities—with different levels of attention and different agenda for each cycle. During the first revision cycle their attention is primarily directed toward narrowing the topic and delimiting their ideas. At this point, they are not concerned as they are later about vocabulary and style. The experienced writers explained that they get closer to their meaning by not limiting themselves too early to lexical concerns."

From Sommers' work we derive no formulas for how to revise, but do notice that writers with experience tend to approach revision as an open-ended process, where they allow discovery and insights to continue to reshape writing.

Type

Richard Lanham (1979) makes a good case for the value of the typewriter in revising prose: "For revision, the typewriter is mightier than the pen. Some people can compose at the typewriter and others can't, but we all need to type up what we've written before we can revise it. . . . The typewriter distances prose and does it quickly. By depersonalizing our priceless prose, a typescript shows it to us as seen through a stranger's eyes. It tells us what it looks like, literally how it 'shapes up.'" Lanham supports arguments advanced by Janet Emig that sight—vision— plays a critical part in reconceiving and recasting our prose. Using a typewriter— or having your handwritten copy typed—allows you to view your ideas more objectively than seeing them expressed in your own scrawl. This is important to point out to students, who often see typing as what gets done to the final copy. In fact, Lanham even argues, "If you don't know how to type, you must learn. For anyone who wants to write, typing is not a frill. It is essential." Of course, since Lanham wrote this, word processors have become the simplest, most efficient means of creating distance through typing: electronic images of words are clean and infinitely changeable.

Simplify

In *The Elements of Style*, William Strunk and E. B. White (1979) spend most of their time telling writers as succinctly as possible what not to do. What they have to say about revision is minimal but common-sensical: "Quite often the writer will discover, on examining the completed work, that there are serious flaws in the arrangement of the material calling for transpositions. When this is the case, he can save himself much labor and time by using scissors on his manuscript, cutting it to pieces and fitting the pieces together in a better order. If the work merely needs shortening, a pencil is the most useful tool; but if it needs rearranging, or stirring up, scissors should be brought into play." This simple advice early taught me to use pencil for rough drafts, to double space and write only on one side of the paper; such a habit allows for revision by making room for additions, modifications, and scissoring. The same works for typing—and triple spacing is better than double spacing. Word processors allow all this to take place on a video monitor, and vastly speed up the process of revision. Reading *The Elements of Style* won't help you reconceptualize your piece of writing, but it will remind you, as you reread and rethink your prose, of a dozen small things you might be doing in the process of revising.

Start Clean

Alan Ziegler (1981) wrote his book to help classroom teachers teach creative writing to students at any grade level. As a member of the Teachers and Writers Collaborative, based in New York, Ziegler has a wide range of experience helping students learn (or relearn) to enjoy writing. Above all, he is encouraging, stresses process, and doesn't pay much attention to error. For our purposes, what he says about revising "creative writing" is solid advice for revising any piece of prose. Under the subheading "Losing," Ziegler writes: "Once I lost a story, and after some remorse I tried to reconstruct it. Then I found the original and discovered I had improved certain parts, while weakening others. By combining the two versions, I had a final draft better than either of the others. . . . This accident can be formulated into an approach to revision: Before doing your final draft, put the piece away and write it again from scratch; then compare the results." I've done this with short pieces of writing, or with sections within a long piece of writing—and found that the fresh start combined with the earlier draft *was* a more comprehensive piece of writing.

Try On New Masks

Walker Gibson (1969) writes: "our decisions about the language we use are, in part, calculated to present our reader or listener with a recognizable character who is to do the communicating." In other words, our own voice in a piece of writing is usually a "calculated" one; how we write—what style, tone, manner diction we select—indicates who we are. According to Gibson, we don masks of one sort or another, more or less consistently, each time we communicate. Each new writing situation, then, becomes a new theatre and a chance to modify character by tinkering with stage setting, script, lights, etc. We tinker thus by revising, by trying out different costumes, lines, and lights until we find one that's somehow correct for this performance. If we agree with Gibson, that there is no fixed self, no one fixed style, then we see revision in terms of experimentation and play: revising what we say and how we say it demonstrates to each of us our existential freedom to become endlessly new characters

WORKSHOP ACTIVITIES

Pre-Chapter Journal Writing

Use this journal writing time to reflect on your own revision process by writing about one of the following topics:

1. Describe how you go about revising an important paper you have recently written.
2. Where, when, or by whom were you taught to revise? If not, how did you learn?
3. How do you help your own students learn to revise papers which you assign them to write?

Post-Chapter Journal Writing

Reflect in your journal on one of the following:

1. Think about the various suggestions of the experts presented in this chapter and write a response to the one that seems most useful to you.
2. Locate a paper which you have written some time in the recent past for which you also have early drafts. Analyze and write about your revision decisions. Would your students profit from seeing how you revised?
3. For a course you presently teach, design a writing assignment which includes built-in revision activities for the students.

Workshop Exercise

Revision (90 minutes)

To help young writers learn the value of revising, ask them to bring to class the piece they wrote for Chapter 3 (p. 45). Ask them to revise it once again, following these specific guidelines:

1. Reread the piece and write a journal entry about possible revisions you would like to make. Don't actually do the revisions now, just write about possible directions. (10 minutes)
2. Select a piece of paper and attach two carbon sets to it and now prepare to rewrite following one of these procedures:
   a. turn over the original draft and start fresh, not looking again at what you started with;
   b. select one line from the original draft and copy it on the clean paper and start from there;
   c. select one of the following different modes or modifications and rewrite (40 minutes) from this new perspective:

- as drama
- as poetry
- as journalism
- as an interview
- in a different verb tense
- from a different point of view (first or third person?)

3. Return to your original group of three and reread your new piece, asking listeners to follow along on one of the carbon copies. Discuss how you changed it, why, and what the new effects are. Take turns.

Classroom Handout

Revision Worksheet

TITLE   _____
AUTHOR _____
CRITIC   _____
DATE   _____

Revision is the process of looking over what you have written and making substantial changes in such areas as organization, voice, argument, thesis, evidence, etc. Revision involves a careful rethinking of purpose and a reconsideration of audience. Think about the following questions as you revise or help another revise:

1. Is the *purpose* of the writing clear in the first paragraph? (If not, why not?)
2. Can you identify the *audience* for whom this is written? (Look for cues in the writing: tone, style, word choice, etc.)
3. How is the paper *organized*? (Look for a pattern here: chronological, topical, logical, compare/contrast, etc.)
4. Is *evidence* used to support generalizations? (Look for examples, specific details, concrete description, etc.)
5. Can you summarize the *main point* of the paper in a sentence or two? (Does the conclusion do this? Should it?)

(Note: Once the paper is revised, the author will need to turn his/her attention to "editing"; see Editing Worksheet [p. 83].)

Teachers Respond

What Is the Hardest Part of Writing?

1.   By far the most difficult thing is beginning—the first sentence, the first paragraph. This is especially true of beginning something new but also arises every new day. I should (but don't always) write.

The other most difficult thing is giving up a manuscript after revision—there are always more revisions, there are always idiocies buried in what remains.

As for the actual process of writing, a difficult task is converting highly technical analysis into comprehensible English and pitching it to a responsible audience.

2.   The kind that's difficult is the professional essay writing, and I suppose what makes it hard is an excess of ambition: I want to do as much, pull together too many diverse strands, think of subjects that are too large and too interesting: I can't hold it all in my mind at once, and I get paralyzed. What's difficult is breaking a subject down into manageable chunks, so that I can do it justice by parts, and then pull it all together with genuine transitions.

What else is hard is visualizing an audience: I know so few people who are genuinely interested in my work that it's hard to picture a genuinely engaged reader; and even getting past that, I don't know how much knowledge to assume: I'm still too callow a scholar.

3.   Getting started. Finding the right word. Sticking to the point. Killing off otherwise good stuff that is *not* to the point. Writing because I have to rather than because I want to (letters of condolence, committee minutes, etc.). Finding that when I have something that begs to be written, I'm somewhere that it's impossible, and when it *does* become possible I've forgotten what I wanted to say.

6
Editing

Editing is the process which makes sure that you say exactly what you mean to say in the most appropriate language possible. Theoretically, it is an almost endless process, for there is always more than one best way of saying something. But for inexperienced writers, who do not yet see writing as a choice-making activity, editing is often overlooked. Yet, teaching students to edit well is one of the most direct ways of demonstrating that good writing does depend on conscious choices. Revision is rewriting at the conceptual level, editing is rewriting at the rhetorical level. Often they go on simultaneously, but for purposes of illustration, I suggest that attention to revision should precede attention to editing. It makes no sense to get the words of a half-baked thought precisely right.

An editor focuses primarily on sentence-level problems, on making a statement more concise, informative, clear. We seldom edit our diaries, journals, or letters to close friends, perhaps because in these documents we are more interested in the rough outlines of our own thoughts than in their precise articulation. But we edit carefully and extensively when we compose documents for more public consumption: reports, articles, grant proposals and the like. Here the outlines of our thought must be ordered and appropriately subdivided.

While I don't like to approach editing mechanically, rules can be formulated for uncertain writers to follow. A number of textual clues often reliably point to words, phrases, sentences and paragraphs which need further attention. For example, the same word repeated several times within a sentence or two can suggest some replacing, collapsing or combining of sentences. A similar clue might be the appearance of a whole series of short sentences in close proximity—most of them starting with "I." Here, too, combining many short sentences into a few larger ones is likely to reduce wordiness and avoid repetition.

However, one shouldn't be too quick to make mechanical rules by which to edit or be iron-fisted in imposing them. Writing by such illustrious authors as Ernest Hemingway, James Agee, and Annie Dillard could well have been pablumized by rule-bound editors. So while we must learn for ourselves what the *cues* are, so too we must be careful to put these aside for good purpose. The problems usually arise from writers who don't employ language "with good reason"; that is, for consciously thought-out reasons. Many students (and, alas, professionals) write awkward, repetitious stuff without bothering themselves about its adverse effect on the reader. They do need rules, at least to start with, so they can learn what the editing signals look like. (One cautionary note: it doesn't usually pay to teach editing through canned exercises unconnected with the student's own work. The lessons don't stick.)

In the next few pages are some samples of academic writing, seven by students, one by a department head, which show common editing problems. You will see that some editing involves simply changing, deleting, or adding a few words, while other editing requires substantial rewriting of the original text. Note that in every case it comes down to a matter of choices. I've presented sentences which need editing within whole paragraphs to provide a context for making such choices.

CONDENSING

The following was copied from a college catalogue describing a Department of Mining Engineering.

> The role of mining engineers is to supply society's demand for minerals in the most efficient way and with the least environmental impairments. The scope of their work encompasses prospecting for mineral deposits, planning and operating mines, processing and marketing of the extracted minerals, and restoration of the land for other use.

A reasonably clear delineation of the department's educational mission. It could use some tightening, however, in the interest of precision and economy. Here is one way to accomplish this, making only minor changes:

> Mining engineers supply society with minerals in the most efficient way and with the least environmental damage. Their work includes prospecting for mineral deposits, planning and operating mines, processing and marketing extracted minerals and restoring the land for other use.

The original passage contains too many prepositions ("of" constructions), five of them, and an inert first line ("The role of . . . is to . . ."), which result in flabby wordiness. The revision cuts the number of words from 54 to 40 and creates a stronger, more direct passage. Other choices might have made other differences; note that most of what I did was delete words and change wordy constructions to tighten language but say the same things: "The scope of their work encompasses . . ." vs. "Their work includes . . ."

DELETING

In the following example a student describes his work as a newspaper boy. I've put brackets around phrases that could be omitted without altering meaning:

> The duties consisted mostly of inserting papers [—that is putting papers] inside of other papers all day long. It was the most boring task I had performed in all my life. During that summer [there was a total of] thirty thousand papers [that] went out daily. [There were] four of us [who] were assigned to do the inserts for all thirty thousand every day, six days a week.

No rewriting was required to improve this passage; many times, good editing is simply a matter of crossing things out. If we had chosen to rewrite, we might have combined the last two sentences, where the writer has repeated "thirty thousand." The twice-edited last sentence result might read like this:

> During that summer four of us did inserts for thirty thousand papers every day, six days a week.

COMBINING

In the following sample, the student begins an essay with a series of stiff little sentences:

> Before leaving for college, I worked as a General Merchandise Clerk in my neighborhood Chatham Supermarket. I worked the job for eighteen months. Initially, I was hired in for three months of work during the Christmas season of 1978. My job then consisted of restocking the shelves with new general merchandise. General merchandise items consist of nonperishable items which a supermarket stocks. Such items are: toys, dishes, clothes, school supplies, greeting cards, and hundreds of other commodities.

The revision here requires that the writer methodically collapse information from two loose sentences into one tighter construction. For example:

> Before leaving for college, I worked for eighteen months as a general merchandise clerk in my neighborhood Chatham Supermarket. Initially I was hired for three months during the Christmas season of 1978 to restock the shelves with nonperishable items such as toys, dishes, clothes, school supplies, greeting cards, and hundreds of other commodities.

Here six sentences totally 77 words are reduced to two sentences and 53 words. The resulting paragraph contains only words that pull their own weight.

COMPRESSING

In this passage, a student describes a battery manufacturing company:

> Johnson Controls is the largest manufacturer of automotive and commercial batteries for the U.S. replacement and original equipment market. It also markets stationary and portable batteries for use in a variety of industrial and consumer applications. With 16 manufacturing plants and 5,800 employees Johnson Controls is the largest of five major competitors and has the largest share of distribution channels in the U.S.

Here the editor must do more than delete. Sentences two and three contain some information that is found in sentence one. One solution would be to compress these three sentences (64 words) into one rather long one (33 words); another editor might wish to keep two shorter sentences. Here is a one-sentence rewrite:

> Johnson Controls, with 16 manufacturing plants and 5,800 employees, is the largest manufacturer of batteries in the United States, making portable and stationary batteries for a variety of industrial, commercial and consumer uses.

A key decision was to omit the term "automotive," which seemed implicit in the other more general terms. Another editor might have insisted that this word was important and kept it in the rewrite.

CHOICES AND OPTIONS

The preceding examples were improved simply by cutting, combining, compressing, and condensing. Such editorial tasks are among the most commonly needed and easily taught. Students should be made aware that editing doesn't boil down to "correcting," but it is done in the effort to make the text readable. If a 25-word thought takes 50 words to convey, what is the net effect of the extra 25 words? They generally obscure meaning and contribute to boredom. In this sense, the simplest editorial act pays homage to the reader's time and patience.

However, there are other, more complex editorial decisions which require quite different choices than these. Consider this opening paragraph from a student essay meant to critique Randall Jarrell's poem "The Death of the Ball Turret Gunner":

> "The Death of the Ball Turret Gunner" basically is a poem about the young gunner who dies and is washed out of the turret with a hose. Jarrell emphasizes the cold this youth experiences in his segment of the war, the ball turret.

As an editor I want more information. I might suggest that the writer should take less for granted and fully explain the work she is about to analyze:

> Randall Jarrell's poem, "The Death of the Ball Turret Gunner," describes the cold, lonely death of a young flyer killed in battle during World War II.

In this rewrite, I have included information to make the passage more complete, while deleting other language more appropriate for another part of the essay, such as the reference to being "washed out of the turret with a hose," a quote from the poem's last line. But the additional information doesn't demand a "rethinking"; it simply offers more information which is already at the writer's finger tips. Thus, this is an editorial act, rather than a revision.

CHOOSING APPROPRIATE LANGUAGE

The following passage reveals yet another set of editorial choices. This student was asked to write an *abstract* of his paper on "optoelectronics"; yet it is apparent that he doesn't know the language conventions appropriate to abstract writing:

> I basically started off my paper with a definition of optoelectronics, and the purpose of my paper. I defined optoelectron-

ics as a field of electronics that has the ability to use light. My paper covered the first optoelectrical component, and the first practical application of optoelectronics. I then introduced the different types of optoelectronical components, as light emitters, detectors, and light modulators. I explained the optoelectrical components as members of these classes. My paper told basically how most of these components worked, and the advantages and disadvantages of each. I also basically explained how they could be used. I described the advantages of the laser, and fiberoptics. I told how important they were to the field of optoelectronics, and what they could or are being used for.

A rewrite of this passage would delete the first-person pronoun ("I") and put the description of this subject in a more neutral, present-tense voice, which might read something like this:

This paper describes the field of optoelectronics, the study of light and electronics, including its historical development and practical applications. Optoelectronic components include light emitters, detectors and modulators; the advantages and disadvantages of each are discussed and the practical use of lasers and fiberoptics considered.

While I won't represent this rewrite as the best possible, given my limited knowledge of the technical subject matter, it does convey the information provided by the student in a more appropriate voice and format with more economy and precision. Editing in this case necessitates knowledge of conventions appropriate to a particular discipline or format.

BEING CONSISTENT

This opening paragraph suggests several editorial choices:

As the liberated women movement progresses, I am beginning to realize my obligation to fulfill some of the duties one normally keeps a man around for. Changing light bulbs, trapping mice, plunging toilets, and shoveling snow . . . things you are capable of doing yourself but trap somebody else into doing whenever possible.

The several voices this author assumes in a single paragraph are confusing. Does she want to write this piece as "I" or "one" or address it to "you"? Each possibility requires a connected set of choices. For exercise purposes I've assumed that she wishes to emphasize *most* her own personal experience:

As a liberated woman, now I change my own light bulbs, catch my own mice, shovel snow and plunge toilets. In the past I believed these were men's jobs and refused to do them.

CLARIFYING

Sometimes a writer will create language that so totally confuses the reader that it isn't clear whether the writer understands the information but hasn't written carefully, or whether the confused writing is really the result of incoherent thinking. In the following example, I'll presume that the writer's problem here is rhetorical rather than conceptual. In such a case I will suggest editing should be aimed at clarifying what is already known:

> Upon examining the question of the goals of the three basic religions that have been studied, I find myself in general agreement with the thesis. Granted, with only superficial knowledge of the three (especially Chinese and Japanese religions), it is difficult to come to a knowledgeable conclusion. However, speaking in generality, the thesis is especially pertinent to Indian and Chinese religions. These, then, will be dealt with first and hopefully, with the most clarity. Since Hinduism presents the most difficulty for me, this religion will be dealt with first.

To recast this paragraph the writer needs to think through carefully what he or she knows, then essentially *rewrite* from scratch. It isn't enough, here, to omit, add, or modify.

> I believe the thesis pertains to the Indian and Chinese religions, but I am not sure if it also applies to the Japanese. Let me explain what I mean, starting with Hinduism, the most difficult of the three to discuss.

The original writing confesses considerable doubt about the subject, but suggests that the author can explain some of it at least. In a classroom essay test, the writer's confusion must stand; but it has no place in a paper written outside of class where editing for clarity is possible.

WORKSHOP ACTIVITIES

Pre-Chapter Journal Writing

Write brief answers to the following questions:

1. How did you learn to edit? Who taught you or what circumstances made you aware of its importance?
2. What are the editing principles you most often follow in your writing? Why?
3. How do you teach students who are studying your discipline to edit?

Post-Chapter Journal Writing

Write briefly about one of the following topics:

1. How do you count student editing when you are grading a student paper? Should you?
2. Design an ongoing classroom activity that would help students become better editors both for themselves and classmates.
3. Review the editing decisions made in creating examples for this chapter. How might the examples have been edited differently?

Workshop Exercise

Editing

1. Select a short prose passage from each of the following sources:
   • a college catalogue
   • a popular periodical
   • a technical journal in your field
   • a student paper from last year's class
   • your own writing
2. Pass out ditto copies of each passage to small groups in your class. Ask each group to arrive at a consensus edit for as many of the five samples as possible. (20 minutes)
3. Call the whole class together and compare the editorial decisions. Point out the difference between "more or less appropriate" language and "right vs. wrong" language. (20)
4. Conclude with a consensus list of guidelines for editors to keep in mind when editing each other's work.

Classroom Handout

Editing Worksheet

TITLE   _____
AUTHOR   _____
CRITIC   _____
DATE   _____

Editing is the process of fine-tuning one's writing. In transactional writing, belief and clarity are essential: a carefully revised paper will have all the necessary components for creating belief. A carefully edited paper will make that clear. In editing, a writer pays attention to sentence-level matters of word choice, tone, economy, and precision. Think about the following questions as you edit:

1. Do you use *active verbs* wherever you can? (Do you "decide" rather than "make a decision"?)
2. Have you cut all the *dead wood* from your sentences? ("It is interesting to note that editing is easy.")
3. Do you have good reasons for using *passive constructions*? If not, make active. ("The liquid was poured into the test tube by the chemist.")
4. Can you use a *smaller word* where you have used a big one? ("Can you utilize this worksheet?")
5. Have you used the most *precise word* or term that you can? (Will your audience understand it?)
6. Do you find any *clichés* in your sentences? ("Can you cut through the red tape and get on the ball?")
7. Can you *combine* any sentences to avoid repetition? ("The water is brown. It is flowing fast. It is polluted.")
8. Do you have any one-sentence *paragraphs*? Should you?
9. Are your *references, documentation*, and *calculations* complete and precise?
10. Have you proofread the paper for *punctuation, spelling*, and *typos*?

Students Respond

How Do You Make Your Writing Better?

1.   The best way to make a piece of writing better is to write it several times. I have often found on Young Author's Day when we are asked to go back and re-write a piece we did earlier in the year I can improve it greatly by changing it around using better words to give feeling to what I'm saying. New leads and conclusions help also.

Leaving a piece is a good way also to improve it by getting away from it for a few days. You can come back to it with a more objective attitude noticing things that need fixing. Asking someone else to read your paper is good also. They can give you suggestions on how to improve it. Of course presentation (how it looks) is important.

2.   I would first look at my paper and see what is good and the parts I would like to change. Then I'll sit down with the part to improve and think about it. Why I wrote it in the first place. Then I'll start to change it. Maybe I was too repetitive or totally got off the subject I'm trying to say. I do that sometimes. Then I look at the grammar, make sure that it is the best I can do, try to change some words (look up in the thesaurus), check my spelling. I want to make my paper as interesting as possible not just to me but others.

I might just have to change a few words but it might make a real big difference. Then I'll reread again and have some one else read it. If there is still parts I don't like, I'll try to change it so everything comes together into a good paper.

3.   I first proofread a paper. I make sure that each paragraph has a topic sentence. Each topic sentence should in some way be related to the main topic of the paper, and they should be in a logical order. I make sure the paragraphs are centered around the topic sentence—if they aren't, I rewrite the sentences that aren't related. I break up run-on sentences and I combine short, choppy sentences. I change repetitive words by using a thesaurus to find new, interesting words—hoping to add spice to the paper. I try to eliminate the number of "ands" that I use. The paper should be smooth, organized and understandable—Anyone should understand the paper, even if they know nothing about the topic.

4. How to write better? That's a hard question because I don't always try to improve my writing. Once I decide that what I have written is my finished copy I say "done" and I put it away for good. I really should try to make my writing better. Maybe I should look at my short sentences and lengthen them. Maybe they are too cut and dry. I know I need some suspence builders, not just here's the facts. My writing is OK I guess. I need to write better conclusions. I should take sections of each paragraph—the main point and put it all together in a conclusion. I just try to get it all done too fast once I reach the conclusion. I am glad I am writing some papers.—But only short ones. I hate term papers. I really like to write just what I want to write about.

7
Research Writing

The assignment most cherished by teachers and feared by students is the research paper. Teachers value them because such papers ask students to perform a variety of significant intellectual tasks, both conceptual and rhetorical, which help them learn more about their course of study. Students may dislike research papers because they are hard work, but just as often they dislike them because they perceive library research as dull, the act of writing as perfunctory, and the teacher's evaluation as arbitrary. In view of the many good reasons for assigning research papers and the often bad response engendered by them, our task as concerned teachers is to create assignments which highlight the good reasons and diminish the bad vibrations, making sense to both instructor and student.

Many composition textbooks discuss the mechanics of writing research papers: how to use the library, write note cards, make outlines and cite sources. Therefore, we won't get into much of that here. Furthermore, conventions may differ slightly from discipline to discipline, so that teaching the mechanics is best left to teachers in particular fields of study. Finally, most high school and college teachers are already over-familiar and bored with the mechanics of research writing. Therefore, I'd like to talk about research writing from a different view, one that perhaps won't work all the time, but will expand conventional wisdom about what such assignments can accomplish.

WHY RESEARCH?

To begin, look closer at the reasons why research papers (or term papers, or formal reports) are a major staple in the academic diet. At best, such assignments ask students (1) to think through their interests and concerns in a given area, (2) to formulate a problem or question of a particular interest, (3) to discuss the question with the teacher, which calls for personal interaction, (4) to look in places, both familiar and arcane, for answers or solutions, (5) to use informational indices and catalysts, (6) to practice the art of skimming to glean pertinent information, (7) to master taking and organizing condensed notes, (8) to refine and reconceptualize the original problem as new information leads, perhaps, to new questions, (9) to integrate disparate pieces of knowledge in some coherent conceptual framework, and (10) to compose the whole into a report that provides some solution or answer to the questions posed—which task, itself, brings to bear all the student's accumulated rhetorical skills and gives practice in the composing process.

Any assignment that asks students to perform the activities outlined above might justly be called central to what learning is all about. When they first attempt to perform research, students may not do so well; as they work at it, through both high school and college, they become better at it—better investigators, conceptualizers, critics, writers. In short, they become better thinkers and communicators. This is the process—or a variation of it—which helps shape the intellectual faculties of the leaders in our society, the *raison d'etre* of higher learning as we know it today. When teachers and currricula work as they are supposed to, students learn higher-order thinking skills that will color the way they receive, process, formulate and communicate ideas the rest of their lives. And at the heart of this process rests the research assignment. So the reasons we ask students to go through this investigative hoop, over and over again, are sound ones. But, some research assignments work a lot better than others.

WHAT MAKES A GOOD RESEARCH ASSIGNMENT?

The elements which make up a truly good assignment are not very mysterious. All you have to do is remember when last you really got involved in or excited about some research of your own. For example, the project must have had some personal interest, either before you began or soon after, for you to have spent time and energy on it; you were genuinely interested in the outcome. As a consequence, it must have been a real question, that is, one to which the answer was not already known, at least by you, so that your investigation had a validity and purpose beyond mere exercise. The project was also one you were capable of doing, given your skills, resources, and energy. And probably it stretched you a little bit, pushed you to know more about yourself. Finally, and this is crucial, there must have been some reward or advantage for doing the project in the first place: money, status, esteem, power, pleasure, knowledge, respect or whatever.

WHAT IS RESEARCH ANYWAY?

First, research implies a question or problem whose answer is of interest. The research involves looking for something, locating information or resources which will help answer the question. As such, research implies a process or method of looking. While this may vary from field to field, the *search* process usually entails having an idea of what can be found and a way of evaluating what turns up. In science research, we call this the "scientific" method and employ microscopes, computers, telescopes, and test tubes to help us find answers; in the humanities, we might call it "criticism" and usually confine ourselves to the study of texts. In each case, along with having a question, we also need a method for answering, one which we can trust to yield useful results.

Furthermore, we need to know where we can look most profitably for answers. School research projects most commonly rely on libraries or laboratories, though we know that in the true spirit of research, our whole social, physical and cultural environment is both library and laboratory.

Finally, research implies a searcher, someone to pose questions, formulate hypotheses (ideas), look for and test solutions—in science research, the all-but-invisible specialist; in the humanities, perhaps, a center-stage Sherlock Holmes bringing his analytical intelligence to bear on a muddle of disparate clues. Either way, the intelligence of the researcher controls and guides the search for solution. This understanding, that the researcher must be in control, as a master interrogator or detective, is crucial to giving the research project integrity and worth.

PERSONAL EXPERIENCE

Authentic research begins with yourself, with your curiosity to find something out. In your quest, you may pose particular questions, look to people and libraries for help, try various methods of solution. But always you are present as the guiding curiosity and controling intelligence of your project. As a personal voice, too. Consider, for example, the voice of the researcher in these two statements: (1) "Two ounces of sulfuric acid were poured into the test tube." (2) "I poured two ounces of sulfuric acid into the test tube." The first statement seems more objective, because of the use of the passive voice and its emphasis on action rather than actor. The investigator is trying to keep a low profile, observing a convention. So be it, *someone* is pouring that acid. The second statement provides more information because it includes the agent of the action.

Talk to your students about their presence in a research assignment—how and when they may wish to diminish it; how at other times it needs to be asserted. In the next four sections, look for the researcher. Ask yourself what his or her presence contributes—do you like finding the person who is doing the writing?

FINDING INFORMATION

The remainder of this chapter will discuss four basic sources for answering questions, sources relevant to both personal and academic quests.

People

Ken Macrorie (1980) says that when you start a research project, start with people. It's good advice. People are living, current resources that tell you who to see, where to go, what books to read (and why), find you shortcuts, ask you questions. High schools and colleges are full of helpful people; so are factories, retail shops, and city parks. In other words, experts are anywhere. One expert will lead you to another, and that one to another, and soon you're bound to make some key discoveries.

Recently I moved across country and bought a new house. My Vermont banker said, "Slow down. Interest rates are high now, but they'll fall by October," and she explained why. My Michigan banker said, "Buy that house as soon as you can; rates will be up in September," and gave me his reasons. My father, an informal source of considerable financial wisdom, was cautious: "It all depends . . ." and handed me *The Wall Street Journal*, which suggested that maybe everybody was right: "It all depends where the banks get their money." And there you have it, advice by experts about a crucial decision in my life: they point in different directions, hedge their bets, but essentially define some of the limits of my question and provide me with reasons and terminology to help me go further in one direction or another.

Were I writing a research report about purchasing a house I would interview the bankers and take good notes. Since both are Vice Presidents, they should be especially authoritative, and it would look good in a paper to quote such authorities. I probably wouldn't quote my father. His value would be as a source pointer or guide, directing me to other sources, in this case, *The Wall Street Journal.*

The best resources to start with are people, and they can be used as formally or informally as necessary. If your students want to use what people say as part of their research material, they need to learn interview techniques. Much of what I've learned about interviewing has come from television: watching Mike Wallace (*60 Minutes*) ask tough, leading questions, or Dick Cavett (*Dick Cavett*) laugh while consulting his notes, or Barbara Walters (*ABC News*) smile warmly as she deftly presses for a better answer, or Dennis Wholey (*PBS LateNight*) say, "Gee, you really think so?" If students plan to use people as documentable resources, suggest that they watch the good interviewers and see how they work. Practice interviews with classmates are also useful and turn up interesting information.

Following are some suggestions for students:

To Record or Not to Record.   With the permission of your subject you can tape record, but the trade-off for accuracy is sometimes extra tension for both of you and a time-consuming replay and transcription. Many good reporters, even when they have a tape recorder as backup, take quick but careful notes in a steno pad (small, fast flipping, unobtrusive, easy to hold on your lap). It helps to devise a few shorthand tricks—abbreviations for common terms, initials where clear, and standard symbols like "w/" and "&." Notes remind you what was said, both during the interview and later and help you frame further questions as your subject is speaking. Even if you tape, make your pen and paper work for you.

Know Your Subject.   This isn't a contradiction: it pays to do some elementary homework about both the subject you want to discuss and the person with whom you will talk. Sometimes this means a quick check in a dictionary or encyclopedia just to learn some terms to help you ask good questions; sometimes it means asking other people about your interview subject in advance; sometimes it means reading his or her book. Keep in mind that you'll get one kind of information if you present yourself as a novice, and another kind when you appear somewhat knowledgeable (see ABC's Ted Koppel).

Questions and More Questions.   Prepare a few key questions in advance. Then plan to follow these questions rapidly with further questions that get at what you want. Unless the subject is quite experienced with the process, she can lose track of your question as she formulates her answers. A brief follow-up question will put you both back on the rails: "What, exactly, do you mean by that?" or "Could you expand on that just a bit more?"

Leading/Open Questions. The best interviewers have a variety of questions: at times they will ask sharp, pointed questions to lead to a particular answer: "Did you erase the tapes deliberately?" which needs to be answered "yes" or "no." But then the short follow-up, "Why?" or "Why not?" is a whole different type of question, demanding an explanation. One question complements the other, and the skillful interviewer balances the two carefully.

Use Silence. This may be the hardest tactic for an interviewer. Silence is awkward and many of us have a natural tendency to fill it—teachers, especially. But silence means different things at different times: sometimes ignorance, confusion, or hostility; other times thinking, feeling, or remembering. So, wherever you can, give the person some silence and see what happens. If it's hostile silence, you'll soon know it; but more likely the person is doing some mental collecting and will himself fill the silence directly. And often, such silence can draw out rich information which you hadn't even thought to ask for. Trusting silence will get you better notes.

Repeat Assertions. Before you conclude an interview it's a good idea to reread some of your notes to the subject for confirmation or elaboration. In that way you can both double-check accuracy—crucial if you're asking someone about a sensitive issue—and you can often get additional insights which perhaps have been incubating as you talked.

Places

Ask your students to go to places, too, and observe and listen. I ask that they investigate local issues and institutions as much as possible so they can find out firsthand what investigative research is like. I've told them, for example, to visit the neighborhood where the most welfare families are said to live and walk its streets, enter its shops. They should be urged to go for the size, scale, color, light, texture, angle, order and disorder, smell and taste of a place, to rely strongly on their senses to find out what's there, and then to shape their language to convey it, later, to others. For practice, have them observe places close at hand—library or bookstore or student union—and record what they find.

I ask students to look around when they're interviewing
someone in their home or office to find clues that tell more about
the person on whom they are relying for information: the manner-
isms, mode of dress, the office (or livingroom), the books, pictures.
Is the room filled with smoke? Is the lawn mowed? Researchers
should train themselves to look closely and take good notes, so
they have a context for their information. Looking and recording
is searching and researching. Students need to learn exactly what
professional researchers do all the time.

Here is the lead paragraph for a research paper in which Mary
wanted to create a personality profile of a local FM radio station:

> WMPZ did not look as I had expected it to look. Never having
> visited a radio station at night before, I had imagined it would
> be large and dark except for a light above the control board—
> a bubble of light in a dark, hushed world. Of course I did not
> visit very late at night—only 7:30 or so—maybe it would have
> been different later. The lights in the office were all on and
> several lights were on in the control room. The long, narrow
> office section held rows of desks covered with papers. Shelves
> between and above the desks held trophies of varying sizes.
> Near the door I had come in through sat an antique-looking
> AP wire machine, alone and black. To the left I walked into
> the glassed-in control room—messy in an ordered sort of way.
> A reel-to-reel turned, recording; next to it another sat empty,
> recording nothing. Shelves covered the back wall, not ordi-
> nary shelves though, ones divided into tiny compartments
> holding cassettes arranged in an order not quite comprehen-
> sible to me. Below the shelves stacks of records leaned against
> the wall; above them record album posters hung slightly
> crooked. In the middle of the control room three desks had
> been pushed together to form a U-shape, on the middle one
> sat the control board. "It's an old TV board that they con-
> verted," the DJ told me. But prevailing over everything was
> Bob Johnson's voice, being broadcast over the wall monitor.
> Its presence seeming to say "I'm in charge; I own this sta-
> tion; I make the policy here."

Mary has a strong presence here, as she takes us into the station with her. We see the bright, busy, "messy in an ordered sort
of way" place that she sees. She skillfully weaves her own expectations together with later interviews and emerges with her focus clear
and strongly stated: "I'm in charge; I own this station; I make the
policy here." Whatever else she learns about the history and role
of WMPZ in the area, the reader will feel grounded with a strong

sense of *place* as a context for other information. Capturing such an image can work in research papers much as it does in fiction: it makes us remember.

Here is another sample where the writer, Susan, remains in the background, but still manages to convey the character and mood of a place, the office where the weekly student newspaper, *The Cardinal*, is prepared:

> The office of the *Cardinal* is located in the Memorial Union building, the last room on the right straight down the hallway of the first floor. On a Monday night it is possible to hear noises from the room halfway down the hall, it was apparent they were working for the Tuesday morning deadline. The sign above the door reads, "Cardinal"; actually this room includes both the *Cardinal* personnel and those of the *Bull Sheet*. (However they are not related in any way except that they share the same office space and are both funded by the Student Board of Publications.) The first glance inside the room gives an impression of complete chaos, the room being very crowded and clustered with stacks of paper and supplies stuffed in every extra corner and slot. The characteristic musty smell of aged wood furniture is evident and a closer look shows all the files and desks seem to be almost antiques, making the new IBM typewriters look painfully out of place. The walls are covered with various sayings and posters announcing the hardships of a writers/publishers job. One particular poster which caught my eye was a rooster violently shaking its beak saying, "sometimes I'm so confused I don't know which way to point my pecker." This kind of humor seemed to be present to help relieve some of the tension and pressure of writing for a paper.

Careful description is part of good research. The writer who is able to observe people, events, and places, and convey that observation accurately, in language, contributes factual information to the research process. Such careful description of "place" establishes living, colorful, memorable contexts for all sorts of inquiries. Ask students to practice looking closely at what they often may take for granted and see whether or not they can capture what they observe in language. Answering research questions isn't necessarily a bookish activity; often it takes place in physical settings that students can visit, learn about, and replicate in their writing.

Experiments

I ask students to conduct simple experiments which provide firsthand knowledge about certain issues. For example, instead of asserting that "most biology majors are really pre-med students" because his two roommates happen to be, a student should enlarge the sample and collect some data: survey a good-sized biology class and find out how many are planning to attend medical school. Instead of saying that automobiles never stop at the stop sign at the foot of Beacon Street, the researcher might sit there for a morning and record full stops, rolling stops, and no stops for a period of two hours; then she can say something based on direct knowledge.

The point is obvious: very simple experiments can yield all sorts of data once students understand how to collect it. There is a vast literature on designing surveys and questionnaires; furthermore, many social science or education professors are skilled practitioners of this sort of observational or opinion-based research. Students should tap these university resources and learn to generate more of their own information—depending, of course, on needs, time and energy.

Texts

Books, periodicals, and other media sources (film, radio, and TV) are the most pervasive, respected, and misused of all research resources. For some research paper assignments, written texts are indeed the best and most accessible source of information. Many research handbooks dwell exclusively on using printed, micro-filmed, or microfiched resources for research writing, and many teachers ask exclusively for written resources. Very briefly, I'll suggest how to tell students about what is available.

Texts at Home

Remember the resources close at hand. Students and their roommates, friends or parents have collected all sorts of books that are within easy reach and can become reliable research starters. Among the most common home resources will be encyclopedias and dictionaries. These, while general, can almost always help students get started searching for something or brief them before they interview somebody. In other words, encourage students to collect and practice using their *own* reference resources.

Encyclopedias and dictionaries are the easiest books in which to find information. They are also quite general and thus most often useful at the start of a search. Encyclopedias like the *Collier's*, *Columbia*, *Britannica*, or *Americana* are commonly found at home. The one-volume *Columbia Encyclopedia* is handy for quick first checks. As you might expect, however, it's more useful with topics that don't change drastically year to year than with those that do. On geographical questions, for example, there is more lasting information under physical geography than under political geography, which changes year to year. Encyclopedias are especially useful in providing context, background, and initial clues, and by consulting similar entries in different sets, students can gain a brief and possibly contrastive overview of their subject.

Most of us have one or two dictionaries close at hand to consult for correct spelling and definitions. Among the most common and inexpensive for college students are *Webster's New World*, *Webster's Collegiate*, *The American Heritage*, and *The Random House*. I sometimes find it helpful to check several of them to get the fullest perspective on a word. While these smaller college dictionaries don't routinely give as much information as unabridged dictionaries do, several include examples or "usage notes" for potentially confusing words.

Other common home sources include various specialty books that we learn to trust for quick references. Looking at my own bookshelf, I find *Bartlett's Familiar Quotations*, *Roget's Pocket Thesaurus*, *Dictionary of the Bible*, *The Reader's Encyclopedia of Literature*, two *Time-Life* series, one or two on photography and the other on animals, the *Rand McNally World Atlas*, *The Hammond Road Atlas*, *The World Almanac*, *The Book of Lists*, cookbooks, home improvement books and hundreds of paperbacks on all sorts of subjects from golf and fishing to interpretations of the universe, all of them potential research material.

Library Texts

To do good, complete academic research, students need to learn their way around the library, the stable center of academic knowledge.

In addition to the reference librarian—surely the most crucial library resource—there are a number of information-finding resources students should know how to find and use. The most up-to-date printed information will be available in periodicals—popular and professional magazines and newspapers. Books, while more comprehensive, will most likely be at least a year or two out of date, even when first published, because of the time involved in book publishing. You, of course, will know more particularly about sources connected with your own area of expertise.

Next to the reference librarian, students should know the *Guide to Reference Books.* This is essentially a guide to guidebooks; that is, it can lead to the more specialized reference books. With this single source, any of us can find most of the other source locators in the library. Once found, be they indices of *Chemical* or *Psychological Abstracts,* or the *Book Review Digest,* or the *Modern Language Association Bibliography,* and once we learn where the call numbers are located, the library becomes a friendly, familiar resource.

The periodical reference students are probably most familiar with is *The Reader's Guide to Periodical Literature,* standard resource material for most high school research papers and probably the most widely-used of all library reference materials. You can find author, title, and subject for hundreds of magazines (*Time, New Republic, Popular Science, Psychology Today, Scientific American,* etc.) going back to 1900. If you need something earlier than that, you can check *Poole's Index* (1802–1906) or *Nineteenth Century Reader's Guide* (1890–1899).

If students need to track down more specialized information published in particular professional or academic journals they will need to consult one of these: *The Social Science and Humanities Index,* the *Social Science Index,* the *Humanities Index,* the *Education Index,* the *Art Index,* or *Historical Abstracts.* There are others, but this list can suggest to students the number of keys available to unlock certain doors to an almost limitless amount of information.

Newspapers with national readerships are indexed too. The most commonly available is for *The New York Times,* but indexes are also available for *The Wall Street Journal* and *The Christian Science Monitor.* These are especially useful because they provide material appearing at the time something happened, unaltered by historical perspective. And once a story is found in *The New York Times* or *The Wall Street Journal,* the same date can be checked in the library's collection of local newspapers to see how the event covered there.

One of the most recent resources for finding information is the computer. Numerous libraries are now capable of conducting computerized searches of particular kinds of information. Such searches are conducted according to key words or word combinations that the computer can locate. One of the most frequently used services is ERIC (Educational Resources Information Center), which provides access to current information such as papers delivered at professional meetings or proceedings of committees and task forces even before it appears in periodical or book form.

The card catalogue provides information about particular subjects, authors or book titles: what the publication deals with, the author's full name, date of birth and death, publisher and date, number of pages, and where in the library it's located.

But the card won't evaluate it; it won't examine the author's biases, how easy or difficult it is to read, or what experts in the field think about it. For that information students can consult the *Book Review Digest* (1905–   ) for the year in which the book was first published. Here they'll find a brief overview of what critics thought of the book when first it was published and where to locate complete reviews. The indexes, such as the *Reader's Guide*, will also point to places where the book was originally reviewed.

Students need to know what to do when their library doesn't have a particular book and they don't know when it was published. For this, they can consult *Books in Print, Subject Guide to Books in Print, Paperbound Books in Print*, all of which will identify currently published books. Or they can consult the *Cumulative Book Index*, which gives complete data on all books published in the English language. (For foreign authors and titles, consult your reference librarian.)

One could go on usefully at length about library resources, for, even after a year of Freshman English, some students won't know how to get started; and hence an overview such as this one can give students some basic knowhow and confidence. Still, their very best resource is their own curiosity and persistence, their willingness to ask questions of people, indices, books, and machines. The act of authentic research is simply persisting to find good answers to well-framed questions.

WORKSHOP ACTIVITIES

Pre-Chapter Journal Writing

Think about the following questions and write for 10 minutes about one of them:

1. Describe the process you went through the last time you actually researched something—either personal or professional.
2. When, where, from whom, and how did you actually learn to do research?
3. Describe how you teach your students to do research.

Post-Chapter Journal Writing

Respond briefly to one of the following topics:

1. Write your reaction to one idea presented in this chapter.
2. Invent a research assignment in which your students must use only non-library resources.
3. Design a comprehensive research assignment which gives students the opportunity (a) to investigate local resources, (b) to work with a variety of resources, and (c) to collaborate with others in the class.

Workshop Exercise

How to Conduct an Interview (50 minutes)

To introduce research as a lively active process, ask your students to take part in the following exercise:

1. Ask your class: "How do you interview someone? What should you do and not do?" (Make a list on the blackboard of suggestions; add some of your own, if necessary; 15 minutes)
2. Divide the class into groups of three: one to interview, one to be interviewed, one to observe. Ask the interviewer to conduct an interview for 10 minutes on whatever subject will forward the research project. (10)
3. Ask groups to stop and ask each person to write for five minutes in his or her journal about what just happened: which questions produced good responses, which did not, etc. (5)
4. Regroup as a class and talk again about the interview process, this time drawing on the recent exercise experience. (20)

Classroom Handout

Sample Interactive Research Assignment

The Saturation Report

Object   This assignment asks you to join with classmates to conduct an in-depth investigation of a subject and to report your findings, individually in writing to an uninformed public. To perform this task well, you must exercise your ability to (1) formulate a research question, (2) investigate original sources, (3) analyze and synthesize information, (4) write in a variety of modes, and (5) work collaboratively.

Subject You may choose to investigate any subject which meets the following criteria: (1) it should be something about which you can ask at least one genuine question; (2) it must include people you can locate and talk to; (3) it must include a physical place you can visit; (4) none of you must be personally associated with it (yet); and (5) you must all agree it is worth investigating.

Data Collection Working collectively, you must pool your energies to collect and generate information which can then be shared by the whole team. In other words, you will each investigate, write up, duplicate, and share information which contributes to answering the research question; however, you will each write an individual report based on this whole collection of shared data. Divide the research and writing tasks among group members so that each makes an equal contribution and collects several distinct kinds of information. Following is a list of the information categories each team is to collect:

1. *Interviews.* Talk with three to four people directly associated with different dimensions of this problem; talk with three to four others who have opinions about it. Ask pre-planned questions, take good notes, and write up the interviews, being sure to quote accurately and record all pertinent data about the circumstances of the actual interview session.
2. *Description.* Go to this place and describe: (a) in strictly technical terms, something important that you see inside, outside, and in the neighborhood; (b) in personal terms, something that makes an impact on you, both inside and out.
3. *Narration.* Record your personal experience of visiting for the first time this place, person, institution, problem—or whatever. Each of you do this, keeping in mind that narration answers the question: "What happened?"
4. *Definition.* Write out all specialized language, concepts, or issues related to your subject.
5. *Library Research.* Locate information pertinent to your subject in (a) newspapers, (b) popular magazines, (c) professional journals, (d) books, and (e) reference books. If relevant, find information about both the local and national situation. Record all data needed to relocate this information.
6. *Artifacts.* Collect, photograph, or otherwise copy whatever "products" are associated with the subject of your investiga-

tion. This may be information deliberately produced by people associated with your subject or it may be an artifact which yields information about your subject.

7. *Interpretation.* Develop an interpretation of some single piece of information you have collected; each of you do this and share with each other.

8. *Hypothesis.* Develop a tentative theory which would answer the initial question you have posed about the subject of investigation; each of you write up this "working hypothesis" according to information collected approximately midway during your investigation. Be prepared to modify this theory as more data are collected and as you compare your idea with that of your teammates.

9. *Model.* Locate, wherever, some other published report or article which accomplishes an objective similar to that you are here attempting. It need not be a collaborative report, but it must contain the essential kinds of information you are also collecting. Photocopy and bring this report to class at the specified time.

Writing the Report   It should be evident that this is no ordinary college assignment—that writing a complete saturation report requires extraordinary creativity, energy, and cooperation. At the same time, this project will exercise nearly every mental skill you need to survive and prosper at the university. So . . . take it seriously, but don't be afraid to take some risks: the only thing worse than an incomplete or late report is a dull report. Here are some guidelines:

1. *Due Dates.*   Certain information will need to be collected at certain times to keep the class roughly together and help solve common problems. Total time for this project is approximately seven weeks. Here is a tentative schedule to follow:
Week 1: Proposal, initial descriptions, and personal narration.
Week 2: More descriptions, definitions, and some artifacts.
Week 3: Interviews and a good tentative hypothesis.
Week 4: Interpretation and library sources.
Week 5: Data collection complete; models looked at.
Week 6: Complete draft of report in near-final form.
Week 7: Complete revised draft.

2. *Format.*   Usually determined by audience and purpose. Can you imagine an interested audience within this academic community? Academic reports use a formal style, traditional documentation techniques (e.g., footnotes), and subheads for

different sections. Journalistic reports are less formal, use in-text references, may use subheads, may use reporter's voice.

3. *Completed Report.* The final report should include (a) a title page, (b) an appendix with all sources, well labeled, (c) a duplicate copy of the final report, excluding drafts and appendices, and (d) careful editing and proofreading.

Teachers Respond

What Have You Learned in the Workshop So Far?

1. The writing this morning was overwhelming! I leaf through the "research" in front of me and say "now what?" Where do I begin? So I just do that I begin . . . building description—I can change as ideas come to me! I *must* work on this here, I'll have no time to work on it tonight! Write and organize—organize and write. This building is too large; it has a variety of functions all important to certain individuals. How am I going to compile this information? How am I going to put it together so the reader won't die of boredom? I feel like banging all the hangers together in the hall with one big *clatter*!!

2. Motivation. The last session has clarified for me what I have been attempting to "control" in dealing with student's problems in written or oral expression. To use English well is an enormous asset in any field (it is sometimes difficult to convince them of this); to reveal one's own ideas requires an act of faith as well. But ideas worth having are worth communicating. I would like to make the first tasks easier for them so that they will try and gain confidence if they are successful. It is inhuman to ask the relatively inexperienced to do what we find difficult ourselves—they must find an interest and deal from strength, not out of compulsion.

3. One insight I had during the last session was that many of the same problems faculty have writing explain why students experience difficulty with their writing. Perhaps, if we look into ourselves we will be able to see into our students. Perhaps it would be useful to articulate for students our problems and how we overcame them. Students should know that writing does not come easily for us and that one can learn to overcome any obstacles to effective writing. We need to communicate not only our own ex-

pectations, but also our willingness to help students with their writing. Writing must be addressed directly by the instructor. Time should be taken in the political science class to discuss writing by political science students.

4.   I learned to put a name to, or to conceptualize as an art what I already knew about writing. One thinks on paper because complicated thought does not come well without it. It had always been a mystery to me why some people can write and others can't: or why some can organize their thoughts and some can't. I thought perhaps it came from reading and learning by osmosis, and perhaps vocabulary and syntactical sophistication do come that way. Writing and rearranging one's jottings, though, has a wonderful effect upon one's power of concentration, and the final product. But it never occurred to me that students needed to discover the first steps, that it was really there.

8

Writing and Testing

Teachers often ask their students to write to find out how much they know and how well they can reason. Essay tests, as these assignments are commonly called, ask students questions which can't be simply answered "yes" or "no," "true" or "false," or with a phrase or two; these exams require students to compose several sentences or paragraphs, on the spot, to answer questions such as: "Discuss the economic causes of the First World War," or "Compare and contrast water imagery in *Moby Dick* and *The Red Badge of Courage*," or "Explain ethical relativism as a philosophic concept." Students are generally asked to answer these questions at one sitting of an hour or two, and are seldom allowed to use notes, books, or references—or to reconsider and revise their answers at a later date.

Teachers most commonly assign essays when they want to find out not only how much students have learned or can recall about a given subject, but also how well they are able to assemble and assess information, often drawn from several sources. Consequently, essay exams often ask students to analyze or synthesize information or to make a judgment about something. In such essays, teachers pay attention to whether the answer is (1) focused, (2) has a thesis, (3) includes correct factual information, (4) is organized; and that arguments are (5) supported and (6) documented (where necessary). Above all, that the student has answered the question asked and not drifted into digressions. Such, at least, are fairly common concerns among teachers who assign and evaluate essay examinations.

Evaluation is more complicated than scoring so-called objective tests (short answer, true or false, multiple choice); seldom is a good grade on an essay exam simply a matter of an objectively right or wrong answer, as the points above are meant to suggest. An essay exam answer may have a crackerjack thesis but poor evidence to support it. Likewise the answer can be disorganized but

103

include lots of facts. It may even be that good and poor students alike often prefer essay to objective tests, the former because they're allowed to demonstrate their knowledge more fully, the latter because they're provided with a cushion against complete failure. So while essays demand a lot of coordinated thinking and writing from students, making "A's" difficult to achieve, they also provide latitude: you can always find *something* approximate to say on an essay exam, and so seldom risk complete failure.

Objective tests can measure quickly how much information students have learned or how well they recognize and understand certain concepts. And though "guessing" is often possible, these exams usually allow students little latitude if their understanding is incomplete. Nor, being fixed in form, do they seriously engage students in an act of learning. In objective tests, it is the teacher who spends the most time, energy, thought, and creativity in composing, not the student. For example, to pose a good multiple-choice question, one that doesn't give away the answer in the asking, and then to articulate four possible answers to that question—only one of which is correct or best—means that the teacher composes while the student reacts. (This isn't to argue that objective testing has no place, as such tests remain the quickest way for a teacher to test "recall" information, especially for large numbers of students.)

The essay test is quite different, not only because it allows teachers to test "knowledge," but also because it allows teachers to witness knowledge being processed. Essay exams are favored by teachers who want to see evidence of their students' reasoning ability. While it takes some skill and thought on the teacher's part to compose a good essay question, it obviously takes even more on the student's part to compose an answer. Teachers are able to see how the student is thinking about something, how he fashions his understanding or how she approaches her knowledge, sometimes through the dead ends, crossouts, and digressions.

Furthermore, good essay questions actually promote learning at the time of examination, asking students to consider new or imaginative combinations of knowledge, because the essay question can't be answered from a single static piece of information from one book or class period. For example, a traditional essay question in an American literature course might be: "Trace the theme of nature as it is revealed in the works of Thoreau, Whitman, and Melville." We have all confronted such questions in English classes. This one challenges students to synthesize heretofore disparate items of knowledge into a meaningful whole and so moves them toward a more comprehensive understanding. Likewise, a question in geography, anthropology, or history, asking students to compare regions, cultures, or time periods, often sparks a kind of synthetic, comparative thought not required until the moment of the examination or in preparing for that moment.

In the rest of this chapter, I'll look at some particular examples of the way writing for testing works in several disciplines. These examples are presented in the spirit of inquiry and speculation and not as recommendations of any form. As Henry Thoreau once said, "I trust that none will stretch the seams in putting on the coat, for it may do good service to him whom it fits."

ESSAYS ON PHILOSOPHY

Ted, who teaches undergraduate philosophy, let me look over a set of essay examinations he had recently graded. I wasn't setting up an experiment; indeed, I wasn't even sure what I was looking for. But I had a suspicion that Ted's essays would show the relative weight he attached to various aspects of the writing: evidence of careful reasoning, correct facts, organizational ability, or rhetorical concerns. I guessed that he would pay a lot more attention to "thinking" as opposed to "writing" skills, though I wondered how he would make distinctions between the two. I read each answer in a set of bluebooks for "Introduction to Ethics" to see what rhetorical skills the student writer used in her answer. Next I tried to deduce whether or not the student's rhetorical skills influenced the grade. Finally I asked Ted, who graded the answers, to compare my analysis to his own judgment.

In this particular final examination, students were asked to answer 8 of 13 questions in two hours. Each question was worth 25 points, with 23–25 points an "A," 20–22 a "B," 17–19 a "C," and 14–16 a "D." Following are the directions and first question:

> Choose 8 of the following questions and answer them in short essay form in exam books. Read each question carefully and answer it directly. *Points will be deducted for irrelevant discussion.*
>
> 1. Describe *precisely* the relation between the meanings of "right" and "ought" as they occur in ethical contexts. Explain carefully what it means to say that someone (morally) "ought" to do something in terms of what it is morally "right" and morally "wrong" for him/her to do. *Be specific.*

After looking at several student answers to this question, I was able to make some observations about the apparent role played by particular composition skills in achieving a high numerical assessment. Here, for example, is an answer which achieved a perfect score of 25.

1. When we "ought" to do something, it is morally right to do it and morally wrong not to do it. But when it is right for someone to do something, it does not mean it is wrong not to do it.

This essay is two sentences long, with each sentence explaining succinctly enough what the teacher wanted to hear about each term. The sentences are syntactically conventional and there are no mechanical errors. There is nothing, in other words, to detract from the information itself. Apparently its very brevity was a plus.

A second student's answer, which received a near-perfect score of 24, was also short:

1. "Right" in an ethical context means the morally correct thing (action) to do. To say that someone *ought* to do action A, is to say that they should do A.

    Specifically, it is morally *right* to do A, and morally *wrong* not to do A.

This three-sentence answer shows some evidence of revision: in the first sentence, after writing the vague word *thing*, we find the somewhat more precise one, *action*, which he includes in parentheses. It is worth noting that the student felt free to revise parenthetically and that Ted accepted it with no prejudice. In addition, the student underlined the key terms—not a significant act but a deliberate attempt to stress the distinctions, at least. His answer is equivalent of a revised first draft, approximately "correct" enough to earn nearly full credit for the answer. Ted said that the evidence of revision hadn't affected the grade either way: "In fact, the amendments didn't really improve the answer. The one-point deduction occurred because the first sentence is technically incorrect, although the rest of the answer corrects the first sentence."

A third example received 21 points—a good answer, but not in the same league as the first two:

#1 "Right and ought"
Right in ethics must pertain to an ethical question.
    Exp. 1. Is abortion right?
This is different from a question with a definite answer.
    Exp. 2. 2 + 2 = 4
This (exp. 2) doesn't create moral feels or doesn't stir someone's emotions.

If something is morally right then it is said we ought to do this.

By "ought" it is meant that it is morally right to do this and morally wrong not to.

Summary—Right must refer to a moral question. Ought means we have a moral obligation to do something.

In this example, we witness what appears to be more student struggle than in the previous two: in terms of "composition," there is less flow, as each sentence is indented to form a separate paragraph. Abbreviations are used freely ("exp." for "example," possibly "feels" for "feelings"). Here is a student having a tough time being precise: "This is different"—but *how*? And "moral feels" is an ambiguous phrase. Yet it appears that the writer paid attention to organization: examples are given, then explained; the argument is summarized. However, Ted found this organizational structure unnecessary: "Examples aren't really appropriate here. A much shorter, more precise answer would have received a higher grade."

A fourth answer is worth reading:

1. The meaning of "right: is that according to our moral judgments of what action is ethical right for us to do according to societies standards there is a right action and a wrong action in different situation. We have a determ. right and wrong through past experience and gathering knowledge. "Ought" refers to an ethical term is the action we should do in order to be moral right. Our moral standards and obligations set up what we ought to do, not saying we will in every situation but according the theory of obligations we should act in a manner which is morally right.

This *looks* at first glance more like an essay answer than either of the shorter answers we just read. However, this answer is much less precise and definitive and so received only 15 points. Part of the problem is obvious—a rambling sentence style which makes it difficult for the reader to quickly grasp the meaning— both first and last sentence require several readings just to make sense. Furthermore, there are enough grammatical lapses ("what action is ethical right," or " 'ought' refers to an ethical term is . . .") that the reader may wonder about the writer's basic literacy. Curious, I looked at this girl's answers to other test questions and found none marked as low and none containing the serious grammatical lapses contained in this one. Furthermore, she answered this question last in the sequence of her eight answers.

What we see here is most likely a case of a student unsure of how to answer the question, and writing poorly because she isn't at all sure of what she is saying. Ted, too, believed the style to be "a consequence of the student's obvious ignorance of the information asked for. The only hint of knowledge occurs in the next to the last sentence, and even here there are serious misunderstandings, confusions, and inaccuracies. The rest is either irrelevant, inaccurate, or incoherent. These are the reasons for the low score. Perhaps this sample is evidence in support of the 'writing is thinking' hypothesis, in that it provides an instance of the hypothesis' inverse 'nonwriting is nonthinking'."

In looking at the four answers and subsequent teacher evaluation, we might make these tentative observations: (1) simple, direct answers are preferred to complex, indirect ones, (2) short answers are preferred to long ones, (3) lapses in spelling, punctuation, grammar, usage, and style don't warrant teacher comment, and (4) such lapses apparently didn't affect grades. Not that these observations will always be true for even the same teacher in other situations. Ted agreed with them, but added: "short answers are preferred only if they are complete and accurate. How short or long an answer should be depends, of course, on the question. The admonition 'points will be deducted for irrelevant discussion' was enforced in scoring the exams."

What have we established so far? We might note that Ted uses essays in a manner consistent with the strengths and limitations of the form. First, he asks students to write essays to find out how much they know and how well they can argue. Second, he evaluates answers according to how accurate and clearly put they are, paying little attention to style, format, and mechanical correctness. He also understands that confused prose often results from confused knowledge, so that while superficial errors are ignored in otherwise good answers, more noticeable errors in grammar and usage, while not marked, seem to characterize poor thinking. Another way of looking at it: a good essay answer might be like a first draft of a more formal paper which is fairly complete and needs only some editorial tinkering, while a poor answer is also like a first draft, but one that needs profound revision. Ted's comment on this overall exercise:

> I try to design exams (both essay and nonessay) to determine whether students have done their homework by acquiring understandings of important concepts, theories, arguments, etc. I do *not* expect students to be creative on exams (e.g., by developing and defending their original views on contro-

versial philosophical issues), since I consider the pressure of limited time to finish the exam to be inconsistent with creativity, which in philosophy requires reflection, intellectual experimentation, and quite often discussion with others. For this reason, I assign outside papers on topics that emphasize creativity and originality. The emphasis on essay exams is accuracy, precision, and relevance. In grading the exams, writing style, grammar, punctuation, etc. is important only insofar as it evidences the understanding that the students are expected to have or betrays a lack of that understanding.

Little can be taught through testing about *how* to write better, while much can be revealed about what the student knows and how he or she thinks. This one-shot, high-pressure medium reveals more about memory and reasoning ability than composing skill—and nothing about finished, carefully edited writing. In fact, those students who approach writing as a painstaking craft may have particular difficulties with essay exams. Students who write essay exams often enough probably get better at it; they learn to display knowledge fully, succinctly, and directly.

ESSAYS ON MUSIC HISTORY

Teachers often use short essays rather than short-answer or multiple-choice exams when they want to test students on a variety of tasks at the same time. Such essays require, along with factual recall, a combining or explaining of ideas. Here is a four-part essay question from a music history course; each part is worth 10 points:

> (40%) 3. Each of the following is a philosophy or musical practice which is significant to the development of twentieth century music. Explain each, including composers who were influential to its development.
> - Impressionism
> - Composition with twelve tones
> - Neoclassicism
> - Electronic music

These four short essay answers to the third term, "Neoclassicism," demonstrate the range of information and style allowable in 10-point responses:

Essay 1

Neoclassicism—Stravinsky. A revolution against romantic
music. A return to the style and ideas of classical music,
but a 20th century skirting intellectual music. For the sake
of the sound not to evoke emotion or imagery.

Essay 2

Neoclassicism—a form used in the late 19th and earlier 20th
centuries. Use of Atonality, heavy disonnances characterized best by Ivor Stravinsky and his two works we are
most familiar with Rite of Spring and Symphony of Psalms.

Essay 3

Neoclassicism—Neoclassicism is the musical style, associated
primarily with Stravinsky, which looks back to the classical
masters (Mozart, Haydon, et al.) for its inspiration. Though
the neoclassicists avoided quite often the introduction of
tonality to their works, yet they were greatly interested in
coherent, conscious "form" in music, stressing the intellectual, objective, nonemotional aspects of art.

Essay 4

Neoclassicism—Music for the intellect, not written to provoke
emotions. Stravinsky was strong in developing this type of
music.

Three of these brief "essays" rely heavily on sentence fragments to convey the information: both essays 2 and 4, in fact, are
composed of one fragment and one sentence each. Essay 3, however, relies on complete sentences: instead of writing "Stravinsky,"
the student uses nine words to complete essentially the same
thought: "Neoclassicism is the musical style associated primarily
with Stravinsky." This student also carefully qualifies his answers:
"associated primarily with" and "avoided quite often," whereas
the other writers make more absolute—and therefore more ques-
tionable—statements.

For comparison's sake, here is a response the instructor considered too brief and deducted 3 points:

Neoclassicism—use of old techniques to organize 20th century music. (Stravinsky)

In other words, brevity has its limits—one fragment does not an
essay answer make.

Is it an accident that the most thoughtful—because most carefully qualified—answer is the one written as a more-or-less whole, complete piece of discourse? Perhaps. But it is also possible that teachers who request full, rhetorically complete answers will get them—and perhaps, at the same time, set slightly higher expectations for prose performance than those who accept any form of response. Here, we are not talking about spelling and punctuation errors; rather we are suggesting that the requirements to complete whole sentences more carefully may accustom the students to complete whole thoughts more carefully.

ESSAYS ON POLITICAL SCIENCE

This last set of essay exams attempts to do something a bit different from the philosophy and music exams we have just read. Harold, who teaches political science, uses essay exams for half of his final exam. The first part is matching and multiple choice, the second, weighted equally, is essay. In a sophomore college course, "Current International Tensions," Harold asked the students to role-play a U.N. mediator and write their answer to a particular question, assuming his point of view. Here is an essay question which specifies a rhetorical context: a situation, an audience, and a purpose.

> You are the ambassador from Vanatu (formerly, the New Hebrides). As one of the two newest delegates to be seated in the U.N. (at the October, 1981, session), you are being interviewed this morning on NBC-TV's "Today" show. [Respond to the following question:]
> "I would like to place you in a most delicate, hypothetical situation: picture yourself as an ambassador from a disinterested nation—say, your own Vanatu—and you are asked to act as an *intermediary* in the present Israeli-P.L.O. crisis. *How would you approach that problem if you were so invited to act as an arbitrator?*" Again, you respond to the interviewer's query. (*Note:* Remember, you are from a Pacific-area nation, *not* from the United States, an Arab nation, or Israel!)

A look at several student answers to this question will indicate to what extent this additional task (role-playing) modifies what the instructor looks for or allows the student more latitude. Again, this detailed look at one question doesn't prove a point so much as indicate a context from which to raise questions about how we assign and evaluate writing meant to test knowledge.

Each of these answers was worth a maximum of 20 points. One student wrote the following, for which he received 17 points (B+):

> The Palestinian-Israeli crisis can be approached as it is approached today by Phillip Habib. Although he represents the U.S. and works to its interest, his negotiations were relatively successful. Some of the steps he followed in his negotiations are:
>
> 1. He used efficiently the pressure on both parties to obtain many compromises.
> 2. He negotiated with both allies to the U.S. although there were enemies. (Considering his nation's interest in Israel without ignoring its interest in the Arab world.)
> 3. He was prudent and showed the strength and imagination of his nation.
>
> Dealing with this crisis was and will never be an easy matter. But the main element needed to have an endless peace in that area is to understand both parties' needs and to compromise and compromise. Both claims to the land must be considered and the land must be divided between them or shared.
>
> So an intermediary from Vanatu must study all the facts relevent to this situation and be as prudent as possible. He could follow Habib's steps but he won't have the Israelis or the Arabs as allies. This would reduce his negotiative strength but a strong and imaginative personality can fill in. His main weapon in these negotiations is to obtain many compromises from both sides.

Certain rhetorical and stylistic features characterize this essay writing. First, it is quite readable, given its three-paragraph structure and enumerated points. Second, the writer establishes a context from the beginning which holds the answer together (the approach "by Phillip Habib"). Third, he makes clearly distinguishable points in each paragraph. Fourth, he has little difficulty with the mechanics of conventional language. However, there is no evidence of the role-playing his professor asked for: the writer maintains the third-person point of view throughout, making no apparent attempt to develop a role-playing persona. This hasn't affected the grade, however.

Here is another answer for which the student received 16 points, about the same B-level competence as in the previous answer:

Well, Mr. Brokaw, it should be said first that just because we, Vanatu, are not directly involved in the present day conflict we can hardly be called disinterested. Our nation has, even while we were New Hebrides, always been interested in world peace and shall always continue to strive for this world goal.

But to answer your question more directly I would begin by directly researching the history of the conflict. It is only through our past histories that we can seek to correct mistakes and not repeat mistakes of the past.

Of course in a situation like this one the gravity of the matter would necessitate going directly to the area in question for talking to representatives of each side. Once each side or nations long range goals are determined, it is easier, and I did not say *easy*, to bring both sides closer together and possibly strike out an agreement. One must also look and find out why these people are presently in power. The question of what determined their power must be answered for a better understanding of their present position and their present mandate.

I would seek direct peace talks between both sides for face to face communication is the best way for an issue to be settled. Failing that I would strive for a representative of each government to negotiate and if that process was not a success I would directly arbitrate the matter to and from each side myself.

This situation between the P.L.O. and Israel is a delicate one and were I to be called in it would tax my diplomatic skills, as it would anyones, probably to the limit. But this is the profession I have chosen and I surely would be up for the challenge.

From the start it is obvious that this student wants to work within the specified rhetorical context. He is being deliberately conversational and at the same time *adding* to the role-playing game: Tom Brokaw, the NBC news anchor who was then the "Today" show host, is a figure not specified in the game by the professor. Second, we find a fair amount of essay-answer space devoted to maintaining this conversational role. Note, for example, the start of the second paragraph ("But to answer your question more directly . . .") and the continuation of the "I"/"we" point of view. Indeed, this writer has a flair for role-playing. Third, the essay is highly readable, using five paragraph breaks to set off his points. Fourth, the mechanics of the language are more or less conventional. This is a somewhat more enjoyable answer than the first one, but it is also obvious that the cleverly devised persona scores more points than do his specifics.

Look now at a third student who did not write as well as the first two:

> Again, I would start with finding out more of the goals and thoughts involved of all the parties. This includes more than just the Israeli and P.L.O., but all the groups in the area. You must also know that this areas history is very old and the differing conflicts go back centuries. Where are the final goal to be so many of the goals are so far apart that there is no common ground between them. You cannot just look back to 1967 and say that is the way it should be or back to 1912. No matter where you look in history (and the history we look at may not be the true history) a different picture is seen. We can not just pick one of these pictures and set that as our goal. That is going backwards in time and all other aspects as well, and no one can see the future to know what the goal should or should not be. The goals that are being strived for now will not settle the area of trouble. They seems that they may set a low in the present activity but they are still not a final answer and I don't know if there ever will be one. I am sorry if I could come up with all the answers to how to solve the conflict, but I am human and do not know all there is, let along to know enough to solve the problems between the Israeli-P.L.O. conflict. But I assure you if I ever do come up with the answer I will do my best to the them know what is is. Good day.

In this answer, the student role-plays, as asked, but appears to use the role as a mask for uncertainty. Note especially that the opening passages do more historical rambling than is necessary while the closing sentences quite literally apologize for a certain amount of ignorance. The role played here is not as informed as in the previous example. It is also less readable, partly because of flawed syntax, partly because it is all one paragraph.

A look at one more student answer might be instructive. In this case, the student received 8 points (of 20), a remarkably low grade within this particular set.

> Let me first correct you in your use of the term Israel-PLO crises. This crisis was the result of interference not by the state of Israel or P.L.O. but the western powers. At present even though the fighting is in the Israel-PLO region it does not make it their crises since a number of other countries are

involved from all over the world. The Super Powers their allies, their satellites all are involved making it a world crises and I feel it should be handled in that context and perspective.

The first thing to do would be for the Israel and PLO to disregard pressure from the outside. Because this has been the major obstacle in reaching the peace. Israel is under American and PLO under Arab pressure and both of these are grinding their own axes. It is the stupidity and pride of the Arabs which forces PLO to refuse negotiation with the Israel.—time out!

It is readily apparent what's wrong here: the writer presumes to know more than the teacher and consequently "corrects" the question rather than answering it.

This student's problem is that he doesn't accept the ground-rules. His own personal beliefs on the Israeli-P.L.O. conflict do not allow him to accept the ambassadorial role without strong qualification. His failure here may be as much a lack of understanding of his traditional student-teacher relationship as his actual or perceived failure to role-play correctly the fictitious ambassador. In any event, he is severely penalized for not playing the professor's game.

When asked why he assigns essay tests, Harold said: "An essay question does a better job of getting to the 'how' and 'why' of a matter. Especially in political science, one should probe deeper than simply a 'recall'-type objective question . . . an essay enables the student to improve his *analytical abilities.*"

About grading essays he responded: "While I pay attention to their syntax, I do *not* deduct credit from the evaluation (or letter grade) for grammatical problems. Only if the student is too vague or confusing in his or her analysis do I deduct credit." Finally, Harold explained that in a role-playing situation, he looked most carefully at "how well the student defends his or her position."

CONCLUSION

In each example we find the teacher judging knowledge according to *what* is said rather than *how* it is said. Each teacher seems willing to grant students considerable latitude in sentence construction, mechanics, and even organizational ability; at the same time, clear style does get rewarded—but never at the expense of incomplete knowledge. In all cases, the teachers used the writing to make a holistic or gross assessment of how well the student really understood what the subject was all about. Writing to test knowledge, in other words, seems to put writing proficiency clearly in the background. Or does it?

One conclusion to be drawn from these limited samples is that writing a good answer to an essay question is one of the most demanding rhetorical acts students perform. In one limited engagement, they are asked to both conceptualize and communicate clearly—to engage in some of the unrehearsed "thinking through writing" that private journal writing promotes, and at the same time to convey one clear, unambiguous meaning to an audience, which is one definition of good technical writing. For these reasons, essay examinations are one of the best means of promoting as well as testing both clarity of thought and clarity of expression. They also stretch students' sense of audience and encourage play with language. For the student who is well prepared, an essay test is an exciting act of problem solving: in the most demanding essay test, "problems" are posed for which a variety of solutions will work—which means that each student must do some careful *individualized* and *creative* thinking. Used thoughtfully and flexibly, essay examinations provide a delightful balance of expressive, creative, and technical writing in one simultaneous act.

WORKSHOP ACTIVITIES

Pre-Chapter Journal Writing

Write briefly in your journal about one of the following topics:

1. Why do you give essay tests in the first place?
2. Can you remember the best essay test you ever gave to your students? Or the best one you ever took as a student? What do you mean by "best"?
3. To what extent should you count the "quality of the writing" when you grade student essay exams?

Post-Chapter Journal Writing

Explore one of the following questions in your journal:

1. Compare your reasons for giving essay examinations with those cited in this chapter.
2. Review the essay examinations you have given in the past several years. What cognitive demands did your questions place on the students?
3. Design an essay examination which, in addition to testing what students know, includes (a) student input, (b) role-playing, and (c) new learning.

Workshop Exercise

Table Turning

To give students practice in writing and understanding essay test questions, try the following exercise a week before you give an actual test. (90 minutes, or a class and a half)

Period 1.

1. Divide your class in two equal groups. Ask each group to design an essay examination for the other using recent course content. (15 minutes)
2. Exchange questions and ask each group to answer the other's questions, subdividing responsibilities so that all the questions can be answered in about 20 minutes. (20)
3. Return questions to groups that designed them and have them corrected. (15) Teacher to collect the results.

Period 2.

4. Prepare transparencies of both the questions and the answers before next class. Project both for the students to see and help lead the class in a group critique of both the answers and the questions which generated them. (30)
5. Conclude by asking students to write in their journals any lessons they learned in this exercise. Share sample answers aloud.

Classroom Handout

Following Directions

Analyze: Take apart and look at something closely.
Compare: Look for similarities and differences; stress similarities.
Contrast: Look for differences and similarities; stress differences.
Critique: Point out both positive and negative aspects.
Define: Explain exactly what something means.
Describe: Show what something looks like, including physical features.
Discuss: Explore an issue from all sides; implies wide latitude.
Evaluate: Make a value judgment according to some criteria (which it would be wise to make clear).
Explain: Clarify or interpret how something works or happens.
Illustrate: Show by means of example, picture, or diagram.

Interpret: Translate how or why; implies some subjective judgment.
Justify: Argue in support of something; to find positive reasons.
List: Order facts, attributes, or items in sequence.
Outline: Organize according to hierarchy and/or category.
Prove: Demonstrate correctness by use of logic, fact, or example.
Review: Reexamine the main points or highlights of something.
State: Assert with confidence.
Summarize: Pull together the main points.
Synthesize: Combine or pull together pieces or concepts.
Trace: Present an outline or show a sequence of how or why something occurs or happened.

Teachers Respond

What Do You Look for in Student Papers?

1.   I generally respond negatively. Most student writing is poor. I gave up assigning term papers for a couple of years because I found them extremely disappointing. They lacked a clear thesis, were poorly organized and very sloppily presented. Students did not seem to understand what a college research paper was or did not feel motivated to perform at an acceptable level. I have reached the conclusion that students need more direction or assistance. It's obvious that I must motivate them to start their research and writing early. Much of the deficiency in quality can be attributed to the practice of waiting until the day or evening before an assignment is due to begin the writing process. I have sometimes required students to hand in first drafts or outlines.

2.   I generally read what my students have written for clarity of presentation, persuasiveness and depth/accuracy of analysis. The first two I find generally lacking; the third is often present although hampered by the lack of the first two. So, when I grade the papers I try to focus the student's thought on the point he/she has made—praising, criticizing, elaborating, correcting as appropriate—and then to point out how that point could have been communicated to me more effectively. Often, I ask for a rewrite, frequently after an office conference. Sometimes, if the idea is creative or intellectually exciting, I will ask the student to pursue it further for extra credit *or* to present it to the class. This is an extremely effective reinforcement and it also adds greatly to my own knowledge of any subject matter.

I give a lengthy critique of each paper, sometimes writing almost a page with the grade. In the composition classes, I give stylistic as well as grammatical suggestions.

3. Internally? With some boredom, sense of tedium, occasional flashes of excitement where I find real creativity, synthesis, details—I am happy when I read really *great* student writing, miserable when it's bad.

Externally? Positive, positive, positive—never write or say anything that could be construed as a damning judgment: every comment is always an instruction, a suggestion for a better way to do "it"—"it" = everything from diction to punctuation to evidence to the basic thought itself. Praise anything and everything that's praiseworthy, and define that category very broadly. The only way to make good writers of them is to make them feel good about doing it. Bad writing = block = fear; I'm as much a therapist as I am a critic where their writing is concerned. I'm sure my standards aren't as high as others.

9

Solving Writing Problems

People write poorly for a variety of reasons. Teaching high school or college students to write better, then, can never be reduced to a simple formula: "Do this and all your students will write better." That's magic and, among teachers I know, magic is in short supply. Furthermore, when student writers appear in our classes, they *already* have habits, biases, notions and fears which determine, to some extent, the quality of their writing. Therefore, it isn't always enough that our own assignments are realistic and challenging or that our own responses to student writing are fair. We must also be prepared for students who come to our classes already crippled.

WHY WRITING IS HARD

When I first began teaching at the University of Vermont in 1983, I was curious to see what my students thought about writing and what their skill levels were. On the first day of class, I asked them to write for 10 minutes, anonymously, on the topic "Why is writing hard?" These were first-year students enrolled at a fairly selective school. Thus, they were bright and generally well prepared for college. Here are four samples written that first day:

(1)   I can't write because I can't express my ideas in a way that's complete, interesting, and understandable. I never seem to be able to start a paper and complete it, completing the same idea I started with. I never know how to use words. When I want to think of the right word for something, I can't.

It seems that while I'm trying to write my idea, I just can't think of a way to write it, lose the thought, and end up writing something that makes no sense to the original idea. Then when others read it, they don't like it.

(2)   What makes writing hard???

Writing is hard because I have trouble getting my thoughts together. For me, in most cases, I am writing because I have to, not because I want to. In a way writing is kind of intimidating—the paper just sits there—I'm usually writing for a grade and it puts on more pressure.

Most of the time people communicate through talking. Talking is more natural. You can read other peoples expression, it's easier to sense if you're right or wrong. It just seems that writing is more formal—punctuation, spelling, proper words. Getting that opening line is so hard.

(3)   For me, the most difficult aspect of writing is getting started or getting my thoughts down on paper. I remember writing papers at my old school and it really was a chore. My English teacher would always say, "You have to think and concentrate for a long time before you can write."

The main problem with that is my mind starts to drift and I end up nowhere. I just have to try and write some ideas down roughly and brainstorm, not really paying much attention to grammar or coherent thoughts. But as soon as I write something on paper, I feel that it has to be perfect because it is almost out in the open for everyone to see. I hate to look at my writing if it is particularly bad. I feel that I have blemished a good piece of paper.

My best ideas come from other ideas when I just brainstorm on paper.

(4)   Where to begin . . . what to say?

Writing feels very personal to me. I usually write when I'm under pressure or really bothered by something. Writing down these thoughts takes them out of my mind, and into a concrete form that I can look at. Once on paper, most of my thoughts make more sense; I can be more objective about them. Puts things in their true perspective.

But, at the same time that I'm writing, I'm worrying about what another person's reaction would be to my words. I write a lot of things that I wouldn't say, and its scary to think of someone seeing so far inside of me by reading what I've written.

A lot of what I'm thinking is in emotions, colors and pictures—things that don't seem to have names so it's hard to capture these accurately. I get so frustrated when what I've written isn't a photograph of what I'm thinking.

We could make a number of observations that would hold true for the first three of these. They seemed to view writing as visited upon them against their will. As the second writer put it, "I am writing because I have to, not because I want to." The third writer has, in fact, learned to write, but feels that he's cheating because he has discovered his own composing process against his former teacher's textbook advice. The ultimate irony of the situation is best stated by the first writer: "I can't write"—but does so with clarity. In fact, every piece in that class, save one, was a variation of the theme that writing is hard because teachers make you do it, tell you how to do it, and continually correct you when you do it wrong, which is most of the time. Writing is how other people measure what you know and what you're worth.

Only the fourth piece was different, more like something I might write. This writer felt writing was hard because getting something just right *is* hard: "I get so frustrated when what I've written isn't a photograph of what I'm thinking." Well, yes, so do I! And good writing, too, reveals deep things about the writer—makes one vulnerable—"It's scary to think of someone seeing so far inside of me." The point is that only one student in twenty-four really saw writing as something that could work for *her* rather than for someone else, writing as important and powerful and useful in its own right.

As far as this writing teacher was concerned, my major task had little to do with teaching students about semicolons, dangling modifiers, or predicate nominatives and a lot to do with changing their attitude towards writing in general so they would care about it and maybe learn to do it better. This sample isn't meant to suggest that all students in high school and college write well but have a bad attitude—most don't and it's more complicated than that. However, "attitude" has a great deal to do with the reason many students don't write well. Remember, these were *good students*, and most of them didn't believe writing was important in their lives. How about all those other high school kids who don't go to college at all, let alone a good one? Let's explore this problem from another angle—the teacher's.

TEACHER PERCEPTIONS

When I asked teachers why students had trouble writing, I received some interesting answers, which varied somewhat depending on the grade level. Here are three lists compiled by teachers from (1) elementary school, (2) secondary school, and

(3) college which assess the problems *they* see with student writing:

Student Writing Problems Identified by Elementary Teachers

1. Writing full sentences.
2. Punctuating dialogue.
3. Paragraphing.
4. Staying with one idea.
5. Getting a good ending.
6. Spelling.
7. Using correct words and grammar.
8. Interest and attitude toward writing.
9. Staying on the line.
10. Vocabulary.
11. Home background.
12. Prestructuring the writing assignment.
13. Getting started.
14. Using their own experience.
15. Rereading and proofreading.
16. Summarizing.

This list, created by 25 teachers at Houghton [Michigan] Elementary School, is characterized by certain mechanical items, for example: "staying on the line," "spelling" and "punctuating dialogue"; it is also characterized by a concern with the more personal elements of writing: the writer's "own experience," "home background," and "attitude." Story-telling also seems to be an important function of this writing: "getting a good ending" and "punctuating dialogue." These teachers worried about making enjoyable writing (and reading) assignments; at the same time, they were aware of their need to teach the conventions and to point out error. They felt strongly the conflict between their dual missions of encouraging and correcting.

Student Writing Problems Identified by Secondary Teachers

1. Writing complete sentences.
2. Spelling.
3. Generalizing.
4. Penmanship.
5. Precise thinking.
6. Reading ability.
7. Reluctance to write in certain subjects (e.g., math).
8. Paraphrasing.

9. Paragraphing.
10. Believing that writing is important.
11. Plagiarism.
12. Punctuation.
13. Systematic thinking.
14. Attitude toward writing.

This list from 40 teachers at Houghton High School, who represent a variety of subjects, shares some items with the elementary teachers, but is characterized by a concern with students' negative attitudes towards writing: "plagiarism," "believing that writing is important," and "reluctance to write." It would seem that the fears of the elementary teachers that students would turn off to writing prove well founded; by the time they reach high school, many students don't like to write, for whatever reasons. In addition, mechanics continue to be important: "penmanship," "spelling," and "punctuation." Finally, we might note a concern with "precise and systematic thinking"—which becomes an even more dominant concern on the college list.

Student Writing Problems Identified by College Teachers

1. Attitude.
2. Having something to say.
3. Faulty reasoning.
4. Having a thesis.
5. Understanding what the reader doesn't understand.
6. Value of writing.
7. Rules of writing (spelling, punctuation, etc.).
8. Context of writing.
9. Organization.
10. Revising.
11. Developing ideas logically.
12. Writing like they talk.
13. Coherence (in a whole essay).
14. Being concise.
15. Self-confidence.
16. Ignorance of conventions.
17. Sentence errors.
18. Including irrelevant and digressive information.
19. Using correct references and sources.
20. Writing introductions.

This list by 22 teachers from different disciplines at Michigan Tech might be characterized best by the term "expectations";

these teachers expect correctness, completeness, and coherence from their students. In addition, many items on the list have to do with thinking: "faulty reasoning," "having a thesis," "understanding the reader." At the same time, we find a heightened concern for correctness: "rules," "conventions," and "references." While the college teachers recognize that student attitude is a problem, their concern is generally product-oriented; college students are expected to produce logical, well-written papers.

Looking for some differences on the teacher-generated lists, we can make these generalizations: first, certain problems are more definitely age-related than others; we can expect "staying on the line" and "penmanship" to clear up through simple maturity and regular practice. Other problems surface only later, when new demands are placed on student writers—the ability to "use correct references and sources," for instance.

Second, the lists reveal the extent to which teachers use different language to describe similar problems, a probable cause of some confusion among students. For example, one college teacher talks about "faulty reasoning," a second about "developing ideas logically," and a third, "coherence," while high school teachers mention "systematic" and "precise" thinking and elementary teachers "staying with one idea." This can be especially confusing to student writers who are not confident about writing skills in the first place; they soon come to believe that all writing instruction is arbitrary and subjective.

For our purposes, however, it might be more instructive to look for similarities rather than differences in these lists: What problems do teachers see students having, in one form or another, at all grade levels? I see three: "mechanics," "thinking," and "motivation." (This is true for dozens of workshops conducted with interdisciplinary faculty over the past several years.) Though similar items appear at all grade levels, it is apparent that "spelling," as a writing problem, is quite different from "thinking," and both differ significantly from "motivation."

"Spelling," a specific example of mechanics, is an orthographic problem peculiar to writing; it is not an issue in speaking—not the same, for example, as "pronunciation." In this sense, "spelling" is not necessarily related to the writer's maturity, IQ, wisdom, or knowledge. At the same time, spelling is perhaps the most noticeable and easily identifiable error in writing. Teachers often talk about "poor writing" when they mean, in fact, "poor spelling"—and while spelling errors often accompany poor writing, they are not a necessary corollary of it. The same is often true for other problems with mechanics—punctuation and documentation for instance.

"Thinking" also occurs on each list, in different words, manifested by various deficiencies in logic, development, organization, and precision. Unlike "spelling" or "punctuation," "thinking" cannot be cured by a set of drills, rules, or workbook exercises. In the elementary grades, teachers introduce "the complete sentence," training children to recognize complete "units of thought"; at higher grade levels, teachers stress the paragraph, a more developed unit of thought. High school and college teachers most often teach "thinking" by assigning units of composition longer than the paragraph (the essay test, research paper, or laboratory report), which demand logic, organization, and support until a rhetorically complete case is made to an audience.

"Motivation" is pervasive, complex, and difficult to deal with. It doesn't show up as a distinct trait on any given paper; you can't point with certainty to a word or passage, as you can with spelling or logic, and say, "That's wrong. That's poor motivation." However, it shows in a number of ways: sloppy penmanship, frequent misspellings, illogical thinking, inattention to detail, abundant clichés and generalizations, and so forth. In other words, poor motivation manifests itself in a variety of more visible specific problems.

Here is a brief look at some solutions to these problems which might also cut across disciplinary lines and grade levels:

MOTIVATION

When I teach a first-year writing course, my initial problem with at least half of the class will be the attitude toward writing—not skill levels. As we saw earlier in this chapter, it's quite common for students who can write fairly well to believe they can't. Literature is usually different—*discussing* good books really does appeal to most people, *writing* about them does not.

I can't account for all of the fears and resentments about writing, but I have ideas about a few. Something clearly happens between learning to write in the early grades, where many students truly enjoy writing stories and poems spun from their own imagination, and writing in the later grades, where students are most often assigned expository and analytic tasks. The very switch from the comfortable, enjoyable, creative story form (poetic writing) to the more demanding, arduous, research-oriented exposition form (transactional writing) may account for some of the changed attitude. Writing, like reading, gets harder as students grow older and more demands are made on their ability to reason analytically and logically.

Perhaps more significant than the switch from comfortable to uncomfortable writing modes, however, is the change in teacher responses. Here, colleagues in my own profession often spend more time on "the eradication of error [rather] than the encouragement of expression" (Graves, 1978, p. 18). While some students apparently do well under such conditions, many come to see their own writing as something used only to evaluate or judge them.

At the same time, beyond the elementary years, my colleagues in history, geography, biology, and math may be contributing to the student myth that good writing matters only to English teachers. If they rely mostly on short-answer tests and homework, they contribute by simple neglect. If, however, teachers assign essays and research papers, but don't pay attention to carefully crafted language, coherent structures, or correct mechanics, they contribute implicitly by suggesting that care, coherence, and correctness are the concerns of the English Department, not their own. Finally, if they assign writing, but only grade and correct it, they reinforce the notion that writing *is* used to measure people, and isn't meant to create learning, joy, and self-expression.

We can, of course, look more widely and deeply into our culture and find all sorts of clues that writing is not a valued activity among adult human beings. Technology has played an obvious role: people use the telephone rather than write letters, watch television rather than read, thus reducing the amount of exposure to all sorts of good writing. Both Marshall McLuhan (1964) and Dan Fader (1966) have described extensively the oral culture in which our students now grow up—with the consequent loss of attention to a more literate culture. In such a mass- and multimedia environment, young people simply pay less attention to writing and practice it more infrequently than their parents and grandparents did.

The business world, which so many college freshmen now aspire to join, also provides excuses for undervaluing skill in writing. Successful corporate executives are provided with good secretaries who fix and polish their prose. At various professional and technical levels, writing is seen as a rote matter of filling in appropriate forms and following preestablished models, with little or no attention paid to the power of writing to generate and develop ideas. Professionals such as doctors, lawyers, social workers, and police officers often understand writing to be no more than a matter of aping formulaic models. And engineers, so the myth has it, work with equations, not sentences. In short, students aspiring to such professions may not see writing as a useful skill.

Never mind that some of these notions are based on false assumptions; that we know from the work of Goswami, et al. (1981) that writing ability often plays a crucial role in successfully climbing the corporate ladder; that we know from Faigley and Miller (1982) that both businessmen and professionals report that writing—all sorts of it—occupies a significant amount of time and plays an important role in their everyday work; that we know from the work of James Britton (1975), Janet Emig (1977), and Linda Flower (1979) the role of writing in developing, exercising, and expounding thinking ability, regardless of more public uses. For all the possible reasons why students don't seem to value writing, few of them hold water.

How, though, can we begin to make writing more personally relevant to student writers? Students already know that in many circumstances their writing will be used to measure how much they know and how important that knowledge is, but they must also learn that in other circumstances their writing will bring them closer to people, support them in times of personal crisis, help them to analyze and solve problems, and create joy when their words come out just right. As classroom teachers, we can do a variety of activities, using both written and spoken language, which emphasize these social, cognitive, therapeutic, and expressive sides of language. For example:

1. Journal writing assignments encourage students to write frequently, freely, without fear of judgment.
2. Peer-group revision and editing sessions ask students to read and enjoy each other's work—again without the necessity of teacher intervention or evaluation.
3. Ungraded teacher responses provide students with commentary, both supportive and critical, on the content of their writing, but without the emotionally loaded shorthand of the letter grade.
4. Personal conferences between teachers and each student about the substance of student writing shows students that their written communication can speak directly to a real audience which cares about what they have to say.
5. Invention exercises, such as mapping, freewriting, listing, or formal brainstorming, introduced in class, demonstrate how language can generate ideas to help the writer as well as communicate them to distant readers.

You can also point out that writing is related to their success in both school and work. English teachers will have a much harder time with this than teachers in students' major fields of study.

Some suggestions here include:

1. Demonstrating to students the various ways that you (who teach biology or business or whatever) personally value and use writing in the performance of your job.
2. Sharing your own writing in both rough manuscript and finished, published form with your class.
3. Asking outside consultants from business, professional, scientific, and technical fields to speak about the value of writing in their own work.
4. Submitting some student writing to executives, professional engineers, or somebody outside the school environment for appraisal of both form and content, asking, for instance, "Would you hire someone who writes reports like these?"
5. Assigning case studies which best approximate the kind of on-the-job writing students will be asked to do later on, perhaps including mock student review squads to review and comment on the appropriateness of the writing.

None of these specific activities, by itself, will really solve a long-term attitude problem; however, each will contribute to a climate in your class where writing will as obviously serve the needs and interests of the writer as it does, in so many other climates, the needs and interests of the teacher. Attitude toward writing is crucial: students who value writing will quickly improve their technical and rhetorical skills and so more easily become proficient writers; students who do not value it, won't.

MECHANICS

Good mechanics are akin to good manners. Whether or not a person spells, punctuates, or documents correctly, according to the standard agreed-upon conventions of the written language, tells the reader more about the educational level or social status of the writer than it affects the literal aspect of the communication. The meaning is perfectly clear in "You're letter arrived today," or "Please keep this between you and I." But in both cases another message intrudes: "I am ignorant." Whether or not it makes sense to allow mechanical errors to override meaning and intent, it's a fact that the writer who pays little attention to accepted or traditional customs risks being ignored, even ostracized.

In some ways, the conventions of language are among the easiest things to teach, especially to students who value writing (or its uses in terms of career opportunities). Any handbook of English grammar, conventions, and usage will provide rules and guidelines. Any dictionary will provide spelling and definition help. The simple advice here is: students should buy and learn to use and re-use such books to help them edit and proofread their writing. Still, there remain a few students who, for one reason or another, continue to spell "a lot" as one word, use commas interchangeably with periods, and can't remember to underline book titles. For these apparently recalcitrant students, it doesn't seem to do any good to keep telling them to use the dictionary. For one thing, students who make these "errors," frequently don't realize they are making them until the teacher points them out. The common student complaint: "But I'd have to look up every other word . . ." has some truth to it. Often people who spell poorly simply don't realize they are doing it.

Other students may complain that comma use seems to be rather arbitrary so they stick them in wherever they feel a pause would be helpful—which probably works right better than half the time and so encourages them to keep following that principle rather than trying to memorize eminently forgettable rules about restrictive and nonrestrictive clauses. Here, too, I have some sympathy; some punctuation rules do seem arbitrary while others are clearly changing.

And in regard to the conventions of documentation, there is good reason for rule-seeking students to be confused. One English teacher insists on using footnotes, another wants endnotes, but the psychology teacher wants references. Some English handbooks teach the documentation principles found in the *MLA Handbook for Writers of Research Papers*, while others are based on the *Chicago Manual of Style*. Teachers in the social sciences most frequently require conformity to the *Publication Manual of the American Psychological Association*—references placed alphabetically at the end, no footnotes, parenthetical in-text documentation. To further confuse the issue, the biologist may want something different from that and the math teacher still something else. Nor is it always clear exactly what needs to be documented: English handbooks commonly tell students to give credit for ideas taken from somewhere else, yet the writers of English handbooks violate that principle frequently. And telling students not to reference "common knowledge" obviously depends on the student's understanding of that phrase. Is the Oedipus Complex common knowledge? The death wish? The tenets of Marxism? To cite Jim Corder (1978): "Footnotes are not needed for statements that would pass without question" (p. 428). But what for a young student constitutes a statement "that would pass without question"?

Following are some ideas that may help non-English teachers, by which I mean non-language specialists, help their students to learn mechanics more easily.

1. Encourage collaborative editing and proofreading among students outside of class. Such cooperative work does not amount to cheating; virtually all serious writers rely on outside editorial help.
2. Identify, but don't correct, mechanical errors, and ask students to look up what is wrong and correct it themselves. Don't penalize if such corrections are made promptly and satisfactorily.
3. Distinguish between (a) spelling, (b) usage, and (c) typographical errors. A student who spells *history* as "hitsory" has probably made a typing mistake—a failure to proofread—rather than a spelling error. A student who uses "their" in the place of "there" has made a usage error—for he or she probably knows how to spell the other form, but isn't sure when to use which. A student who writes "relevance" as "relevence" is in fact misspelling and should practice the word.
4. Suggest that students read their papers aloud, to themselves, before turning them in. Or that they have a friend read it to them. Awkward and ungrammatical structures are easily caught this way. (Non-native speakers and those with subculture dialects may not find this helpful.)
5. Explain to the class what you expect in terms of documentation. When I'm teaching writing to English majors, I expect MLA format; non-majors are encouraged to use the conventions appropriate to their discipline. To both groups, I stress that there is a logical concern behind documentation: to establish "who wrote what, and who published it, where and when." That information helps the reader find the source, which is why documentation exists in the first place.
6. Try to recognize that certain so-called rules of language are arbitrary, others are changing, but that some others can't be violated without rather grave consequences. I don't spell *judgment* as "judgement," even though this British spelling is now generally accepted. Nor do I go along with "infer" for "imply," although many people do. As for contractions in all but the most formal writing, why not? Or sentences ending in prepositions. While most of us agree most of the time on what's acceptable and what's not, we also have personal prejudices and need to tell our students which is which.

7. Pay attention to errors in the context of whole compositions, rather than asking students to do arbitrary drills. Research (McClellan, 1978) tells us that spelling is taught best to younger students by studying lists. However, the same techniques work less well with older students and adults, who most often learn in context. Your own students will learn best to correct their own mistakes rather than studying arbitrary lists or doing exercises on conventions they are never called upon to actually use.

8. For students who make many errors, both logical and mechanical, request revision on those which are more important first (the logic), pointing out that later they will still need to attend to their spelling or whatever. At the same time, be as specific as possible about the nature of the problem; just circling or underlining all mistakes or writing "awk" in the margins may not locate for the student exactly what the problem is.

9. If your school has a language lab or writing lab or writing center or basic-skills center, refer to it students who have dialect, second-language, or remedial problems. Usually such labs have a tutorial staff trained to spend one-on-one time with students. You don't.

THINKING

There are no quick fixes here. When a paper is disorganized, lacks a thesis statement, or doesn't support propositions with hard evidence, it may be a case of flawed cognition or reasoning ability. Or the paper might be the result of hurried one-draft writing because the student (1) budgeted time poorly, (2) had a crisis in his or her life, or (3) didn't like or understand the assignment, etc. In other words, it is often difficult to tell from one piece of writing whether or not a student reasons well. This is the problem with one-shot, 50-minute writing samples meant to rank students accurately according to ability. I know a hundred factors that can intrude on any given writing performance, which can make that particular writing product deficient.

But in a school context, where a teacher usually works with a student over a period of 10, 15, even 30 weeks, collateral evidence often develops which confirms whether the conceptual development of a given paper is characteristic of the actual cognitive ability of the student. Talk in class, test and quiz scores, and further written work soon establish whether or not the first writing sample is valid.

It should be evident that talking about conceptual problems opens up so many questions that I can but touch on the issue here. Whole disciplines—philosophy, psychology, and education, for example—wrestle with teaching and studying cognition. At the same time, each discipline teaches a pattern or method of reasoning peculiar to its endeavor—biology, anthropology, physics, history. And within each are substantial variations of doctrine that substantially influence thought processes and methodology—a historian who is quantitative or empirical versus one who is Marxist or Freudian, for example. For our purposes, it is enough to observe that written discourse reveals the quality of a person's thought perhaps more clearly than any other medium, and that the process of generating it affects the quality of the thought so generated. On the one hand, then, writing contributes to the development of thought and on the other, communicates whether that thought is, in fact, lucid, sensible, logical, or developed.

As we examined in Chapter 2, it is difficult to separate conceptual ability from composing ability; the two are intertwined at many points. So, while all writing activities engage one's brain to one degree or another, let me suggest a few pedagogical practices that most obviously encourage, work on, or train one's thinking:

1. *Expressive Writing.*   Teachers who ask their students to do frequent bits of self-expressive writing give their students regular practice in thinking and articulating for themselves, rather than to please the teacher. Whether in journals, notebooks, or on occasional drafts, writing expressively helps people formulate thought through language. Practicing this regularly enhances one's memory and perhaps leads to insight and understanding. (See Chapters 1 and 2 for a complete discussion of expressive writing and journals.)

2. *Multiple-draft Writing Assignments.*   Every time you ask your students to revise a paper again before handing it in, you are asking them to *rethink* that paper. When you point out missing evidence, poor organization, or faulty logic, you ask writers to reconceive and rereason more carefully. When students are asked regularly to rethink their work, they will, in fact, learn to think more methodically, carefully, and convincingly—which is the intent of our instruction in the first place.

3. *Peer-Group Discussion in Class.*   One of the easiest activities to use in small classes is peer-writing/discussion groups. Periodically divide a class of 25 into five groups of five each and ask them to read, edit, and revise, and discuss each other's

writing. Such activities promote cognitive and emotional growth by exercising all the student's learning powers at once: reading, listening, speaking, and writing. The more often students are asked to perform critical functions, without the teacher dominating the situation, the more confidence they develop about both their intellectual and communication skills. In such small groups, they learn to be responsible for their opinions—their thoughts—just as they are meant to be when they write.

There are great numbers of exercises and activities that stem from these three general practices—writing expressively, revising, and meeting in small groups—some of which incorporate all three practices in the same exercise; however, the particular ideas are best left to each teacher's disciplinary and academic circumstances and imagination. Teachers who incorporate some variation of these practices will be asking their students to stretch out and grow.

There is perhaps one additional consideration here. Lee Odell (1983) often asks teachers to enumerate or write the conceptual demands of each assignment they make for their students. What mental operations are you asking your students to perform in order to do this assignment successfully? Do you want students to analyze? Synthesize? Give opinions? Judge? Evaluate? Recall? Odell believes that if teachers examine their assignments thus critically, they'll be better able to anticipate outcomes and also to help students focus and strengthen their conceptualizing.

People have difficulties writing well for all sorts of reasons. Different problems, then, demand different solutions. Teachers who make an effort to distinguish between the paper poorly organized because the student spent 20 minutes on it the night before, versus the one written by a student who doesn't know how to organize information, won't waste must time responding to the first case, but may arrange tutorial sessions for the second. And so on. Being aware of the problems will not, of course, lead to magical solutions, but most of us consider such awareness a first step toward more effective and more humane teaching.

WORKSHOP ACTIVITIES

Pre-Chapter Journal Writing

Do the following sequence of journal writes before reading this chapter:

1. Why is writing hard?
2. What makes it easier?
3. How do you think your students would answer these same questions?

Post-Chapter Journal Writing

Write for five minutes on each of the following questions:

1. What problems do your students seem to have writing your assignments?
2. What have you done in the past to help them solve these problems?
3. What might you do in the future to ease their difficulties?

Workshop Exercise

You might try with your class the same exercise described in this chapter to find out what your students think about the value of writing:

1. Ask your students to do a 10-minute freewrite on the question: "Why is writing hard?" Ask for volunteers to read their answers aloud; read yours.
2. Ask as a follow-up question: "What makes it get easier?" This time make a blackboard list of their responses; the results should be a fairly good suggestion list for writers who want to become better writers. It will also be a rich list for teachers who want to help students improve their writing with better assignments.
3. Finally, ask your students what questions they have about improving their writing. The chances are that some of those could be answered by the group on the spot, while others might be addressed later in the term either in class or in conference.

Classroom Handout

Suggestions for Making Writing Easier

1. Write in a place where you are comfortable and undistracted.
2. Use materials you feel particularly good about: your favorite kind of pen or pencil (or word processor), clean, fresh paper in a color that suits.
3. Plan to write more than one draft.
4. Think positively: make yourself interested in assigned topics.
5. Find the different angle on each assignment.
6. Find a way to have fun with assignments, but cover the bases.
7. Seek feedback on early drafts; get help proofreading on final ones.
8. Ask what you know, what you don't, and what else you need to.
9. Remember: all writing is persuasive; you must create belief.
10. Trust your ear; read your paper aloud to catch problems.
11. Review old papers: What have readers liked and disliked about them in the past?

Students Respond

How Do You Start Writing a Paper?

1.   When I start writing a paper I begin with my topic and think of what I'm going to write about it. In other words what is my purpose or goal of the paper I'm writing. Next, I would think about the person or audience to whom the paper is going to and try to develop my paper to be interesting to them. I would then begin to write my paper and use the opening paragraph to state my topic. If I have time before I begin to write (which I usually don't) I like to make an outline so that I have something to follow while I'm writing. An outline kind of gives me a guide to fall back on in case I get stuck. Right now I can't think of anything else to write about my paper. Oh, of course the topic has to be interesting to me or I can't write anything at all.

2.   It really takes me a long time to start to write a paper. I never know where to begin. I never know when to start. Should I wait a couple of more hours before I start to write the paper or should I start now. English writing is hard if your not creative. My mind doesn't seem to ever want to be creative when it comes to English

papers. I'll procrastinate to the bitter end. Papers should start with a real interesting sentence, if I ever find that sentence its sure to have come upon after many crumpled up papers with just one line on it. Papers for me mean a headache and that how the beginning is. There are always questions on what should be it. It will mean I don't know where to begin. I'll play around with a few thoughts but none of them will ever seem right.

3. I start writing a paper by just writing down anything that comes to my mind. I write the whole paper as one big mess. Kind of like free writing. Then I rewrite it into sentences. And I keep re-writing it until it finally takes some form. Oops. I forgot. I usually write some type of outline first. . . . After that I start writing down anything that comes to mind from my outline. I keep on writing and finally go back and correct spelling, grammar, etc, I always end up taking so much time to start to write it. More than usual. My handwriting is horrible so it takes longer. Usually as I start to write my brain thinks faster than I can write every-thing down so I am constantly writing notes on different papers. I end up with so many different pieces of paper and so many copies. How can a person write on how to start a paper? I can't write this much. . . .

10

Teaching Workshop Style

What happens to your teaching when you ask students to write more often in your classes? Maybe more than you bargained for. If you restructure your class to accommodate student journals, multiple-draft papers, and small-group activities, you may find that you have changed more than just your assignments. You may have also changed the nature of the learning that occurs in your class. This chapter will look more closely at some of the tacit implications of writing across the curriculum.

MODES OF INSTRUCTION

From the School of Education, I've borrowed a simple schema that describes how most of us go about teaching. This schema places pedagogy along a continuum: at the far right is a mode of instruction we might call "didactic," where the instructor tells the students what they must know, often in a lecture format, and the students listen, take notes, and commit to memory the teacher's information or ideas. In this mode, the teacher is active, the students reactive, the learning passive.

Moving along this continuum, somewhere toward the middle, we could identify a mode of instruction best called "guided," where the instructor poses problems, questions, and exercises for the students to solve, guiding them to solutions, answers, and results that teach students lessons. The teacher uses his or her prior training and knowledge to likewise train and inform his or her own students. In this mode, both teacher and students are alternatively active and passive.

At the far left of this continuum is a mode we might call "open," where teacher and students together pose and solve problems, ask and answer questions, and explore real-world issues. Here, the teacher is less concerned with inculcating knowledge or prescribing training than in helping students become autonomous, independent learners in their own right. In the open mode, the students are often more active than the teacher, continually finding themselves in learning situations where passivity is impossible.

Few teachers operate in only one of these modes; most of us who teach use all three at different times. In fact, I am sometimes "didactic," "guiding," then "open" in the same class period. If pressed, however, to declare which mode is most important, I would unhesitatingly say the "open" one, for as a liberal arts instructor, it is ultimately more important that I help students learn to learn to be autonomous and critical thinkers than that I teach them any particular set of knowledge. At the end of a class, I want students to be fairly capable of carrying on further investigations on their own.

Why dwell on something that's obvious to most teachers? Because the writing assignments are closely linked—sometimes inadvertently—to the lessons we teach. You can't, for example, make didactic writing assignments and, at the same time, promote open learning. Mixed message. Yet, ironically, some instructors do just that. Writing assignments deliver important messages to students, messages which either support or contradict the lessons delivered in readings, lectures, and classroom discussion. Here are some examples:

If you are in didactic mode, you will most likely ask your students to copy lecture notes, fill in workbook blanks, take frequent quizzes and objective tests, and, in general, prove to you through recall that they have learned precisely what you had to teach. (Good examples might be memorizing formulas in math or science or learning the dates of Civil War battles in history.)

If, instead, you are guiding your students to certain insights, you are more likely to give assignments which reflect that looser control: you will ask your students to take their own reading notes, do open-ended exercises, write one-answer essay tests, and perhaps do guided research. (A typical guided assignment in my field would be teaching something called "The research paper," where it is more important that the students learn the forms of research reporting than that they discover anything new.)

Finally, if you are promoting open, critical inquiry, you will want your students to write, as much as possible, material that they generate themselves and that you don't always correct. You will assign journals, where students learn to trust their own thoughts and opinions, essays and papers in which there might be several good answers rather than one "right" one, and research projects in which neither you nor your students know the results in advance. And you will trust them to pose their own problems and ask their own questions. Above all else, when you begin making open-ended writing assignments, you begin trusting your students to think and write about topics they choose and care about. They also begin trusting you to read their work with care and respond with some sensitivity; together, you and the class may begin to act more like a community of scholars. When that happens—and good writing assignments help make it happen—you may well find yourself teaching workshop style. It's a lot of work, but once you discover how writing creates community in a classroom, it's hard to go back.

SHARING POWER

Teachers who ask for more writing from students are asking for more student participation and opinion in the class. Writing assignments, even more than reading assignments, transfer responsibility, and hence power, to the learner. When students are asked to compose their own thoughts on paper, they are really asked to think more, find their own voices, and share them. Articulating ideas on paper commits writers to one direction rather than another and helps them locate and assert their individual voices.

When you ask students to write to themselves and promise not to red-pencil that writing, you are providing a personal sanctuary for private thought about academic matters. You are doing more, actually: you are sanctifying the value of personal reflection and affirming the student's right to his or her own opinion about your subject. Expressive writing assignments and journals give students license to think freely about what they want; they legitimize such thinking as part of the academic experience.

When you ask students to write to audiences other than you, the teacher, you are not only challenging them to make some fresh judgments; you are also validating other sources of authority: newspaper editors, local business leaders, school boards, parents, elected officials, other teachers. Tacitly you stop saying that you are the sole source of truth on this or that matter.

Even more important, when you ask students to write to each other and provide some class time for students to meet together and discuss each other's writing, you are giving over to them time to help form their own community of learners. None of this is easy for a teacher used to controlling single-handedly the entire flow of learning in a class.

PEER GROUPS

Asking students to work autonomously in groups de-centers the authority in your classroom. The groups with their several and collective personalities become a locus of authority and responsibility—at least for the duration of the project. So right off you must be willing to trust your students enough to give them their own voice in at least this project. Leaders and stragglers, as well as all sorts in between, will emerge, but that, of course, is the way it should be. Grouping students within a class to solve a problem, answer a question, or complete a project is a fair approximation of how social institutions, including corporations and universities, operate in the real world. Collective problem solving is a real and useful process. Groups gain strength by pooling the resources, knowledge, and skills of individuals to create a more resourceful, knowledgeable, skillful collective entity than existed before. So a group, given a real problem to solve, should do significantly better than a single individual tackling the same problem. That, at least, is what I expect when I ask a group rather than an individual to solve a problem.

Students who work in groups—serious well-directed groups— learn to trust themselves and each other in a way not possible so long as the teacher is the source of all knowledge and sole evaluator of competency. Students who become accustomed to group work "educate" themselves in the very best sense of that word. These, of course, are best-case scenarios, when groups really work. At times they won't and you'll blame yourself when a group is quarrelsome rather than cooperative or bored rather than involved. You probably can't use groups—trust them fully—unless you're also prepared for some occasions where they won't, despite your best efforts, become self-actualizing. If you are careful and thoughtful, however, groups will work well most of the time, depending on what you ask them to do.

Good group projects most often pose real and open-ended questions, as do good individual writing assignments. In history, for example, this could mean doing collaborative research, writing the history of an event, like Watergate, using both primary and interpretative sources, or corroborating multiple assessments to arrive at an independent assessment of what actually happened. In biology the group could be asked to present a well-documented case for this or that policy regulating genetic engineering. A good group project will be very much like a good research paper project. Considerably more should be possible, however, than if a single individual works on the task: more information and more points of view considered, more data collected and more experiments conducted.

The very best project for a group would be one that drew on individual strengths within the group so that the outcome will amount to more than what any single person could devise. For example, any problem or question that has ramifications beyond single departmental or disciplinary boundaries is a natural: and most "real" problems, whether originating in social, scientific, legal, technical or aesthetic fields involve multiple concerns, whether we're talking about profit making, gun control, abortion, highway location, or garbage disposal. Groups of students bringing to bear collective energy can both solve such problems and educate each other in the process.

In my Communications Theory classes, I commonly ask students to "Describe our university as a communications system." They must divide up research tasks on the problem (some do interviews, some library research, some on-site investigation), pool the resultant information, but write individual reports. How students answer the larger question depends very much on the smaller questions they begin asking as they define their individual approaches. They learn to read to each other and critique each other. In sharing information, I ask them to footnote each other, just as they would any other outside independent source. Here is a classroom activity where students become co-investigators and problem solvers with the teacher. (See the Classroom Handout in Chapter 6, page 83, for a more detailed description of this assignment.)

I use groups within classes in three general ways: (1) to solve short problems, the solutions to which will feed into the discussion topic of the day; (2) to answer larger questions, allowing class time for oral reports; and (3) to become permanent writing groups which meet weekly or biweekly to read and critique each other's writing. Any or all of these are possibilities for content classes interested in what Paulo Freire calls "critical inquiry." Giving students class time to talk to each other—and trusting that this is time well spent—is the fundamental secret of workshop-style classes.

The question you need to ask is not which *type* of group you want to try out, but whether the idea of using student groups at all is compatible with your class goals. Such groups, when used more than once in a class, will change your class in two distinct ways. First, you won't have as much time, yourself, to disseminate information and cover material; for the group process to work well, the groups will need class time both to plan and present. But consider that the loss in the sheer amount of information which can be covered will be more than offset by the learner responsibility and, consequently, by the depth of questioning and strength of retention. The second outcome will be a relatively relaxed, informal, and friendly class, in which you can participate more, at times, as a member or chair than as the sole source of knowledge and power. If you are interested in teaching in such circumstances, consider in more detail the three types of groups I have described.

Problem-Solving Groups

Solving problems by talking with other people is both effective and fun. More effective than posing the same problem to a large group of people, because there is more time for interaction, reaction, and followup; more fun because everyone in a small group gets personally involved. Small groups work well at problem solving; we try to make use of them regularly. Such groups help generate better writing because they so effectively help develop a context for it, serve as a stimulus for prewriting, and provide an immediate audience for written drafts. Typically we use groups of three students to get everyone in the class involved in some common issue, allow from five to fifteen minutes to generate solutions or approaches to solutions, then ask them group by group to report briefly on what they have found out. Actually, the real strength of such exercises lies more in the small group working together than on any subsequent report they issue; however, comparing results, group by group, also provides an arena in which to play further with ideas. Following are some of the problems recently posed for my class in nineteenth-century American literature (later in the term these same groups were asked to pose and answer problems of their own formulation):

1. Write a journal entry about your initial reaction to reading Benjamin Franklin's autobiography. Break into groups of three and read your reactions to each other. How similar or different are your reactions? Try to explain the differences.
2. [After passing out short poems by Emily Dickinson; eight groups of three each.] Read and respond collectively to "I Heard a Fly Buzz when I Died." Which lines pose problems for you and why?
3. [After reading "The Fall of the House of Usher" by Edgar Allen Poe; five groups of five each.] Discuss one of the following aspects of the story and make an outline of your findings to the class: (a) plot, (b) setting, (c) theme, (d) character, and (e) narrative point of view.

4. [After reading an essay by Ralph Waldo Emerson; six groups of four each.] Summarize the ideas in the first paragraph and explain how they fit into the essay as a whole.
5. [After reading *Walden* by Henry David Thoreau; five groups of five each.] Generate a list of questions (or paper topics) the answers to which will help us better understand *Walden*. [An extension of this, which would take the entire class period, would be to ask the groups to exchange questions and answer each other's, not necessarily in writing.]

Presentation Groups

In setting up groups to make formal oral presentations to the class, I try to stimulate student imagination by asking a provocative open-ended question, to which there may be numerous good solutions, but that will require some imaginative collaboration to answer. At first this question may strike students as odd or outrageous. Frustration can be healthy, however, and will often generate collaborative solutions. The following examples come from a sophomore class in American literature; variations of these questions could apply to any subject area where interpretation is an issue:

Instructions: Divide into five groups of six each; elect a chairperson and note-taker and develop a strategy for making a class presentation next week on one of the following problems. (*Note*: the whole class will evaluate the merits of each presentation based on how well prepared the group is, and whether or not they "teach" us anything—and remember that we can be educated through laughter and fear.)

1. Outline a plan for Walden III. (Remember *Walden Two* by B. F. Skinner?) Base this experiment on principles derived from Henry David Thoreau and Robert Frost. Make it possible for more than one person to live in this new Walden, which wasn't possible in Thoreau's experiment. Add visual aids of your choice; dress appropriately.
2. Convince the class that it is essential for engineering students to study poetry to improve their ability to creatively solve problems. Dickinson, Frost, and Auden are your resources; supplement with blackboard diagrams.
3. Prepare a demonstration for the class about the importance of images in the world; show how both literary authors and business entrepreneurs alike depend on images to inform, entertain, educate, and convince people. Your resources

include all the authors you have read in this course plus whatever else you can find. (What *is* an image anyway and what does Kodak have to do with it?)

4. As a group, write two poems, one each after the fashion of Robert Frost and E. E. Cummings. Transfer your poems to ditto masters and run off 30 copies of each. Hand out to the class and ask them to "interpret" the significance of the poems. (Do not defend or explain your work; wise artists learn the act of being silent about their own work. Resources: your creative wits and some courage; be sure to sign your names.)

5. Select two authors who in your opinion provide the most penetrating social criticism and point out similarities and differences in what they have to say. Demonstrate to the class that their critiques have value today.

A further note: when sometimes I miss a class during any given term, I have found that students can be asked to meet by themselves, in small groups, in class, library, or union, to plan their presentations. In such situations, students generally use the time well.

Writing Groups

Sometimes I form *ad hoc* groups to read their writing to each other, but more commonly groups are formed early in the term and asked to meet whenever they have a paper to share. I also do this with literature (content) classes, although they meet less often than do straight writing class groups.

In the summer of 1978, I codirected a National Writing Project site. We followed guidelines drawn up by James Gray and James Moffett which required 24 teachers in the Project to begin a piece of writing the first week (on anything they wanted to write about) and continue that piece from week to week for five weeks, changing how they approached the piece from week to week, first perhaps as an internal monologue, later as a journalistic piece, and again as an abstract argument. Participants met on Monday and Thursday afternoons for two hours in groups of six and took turns reading and responding to each other. When the Project ended, most teachers identified the regular writing groups as the most important learning they had done all summer, books and presentations notwithstanding.

The power of these groups was twofold: first, each writer had a real, known audience for his or her work so that the private writing activity became more real and purposeful; second, each writer received regular, honest, and personal response to his or her writing, which generated new directions for rewriting and revision. This same dynamic works in classes meeting three times a week for 10 or 15 weeks as well as for condensed courses of four or five days, during which the groups are able to meet maybe three or four times. Because members get to know each other and because they meet regularly, the groups generate an intensity seldom approached in the class as a whole. Here's how such groups can work:

Students write a draft on a ditto master (or photocopy it) and distribute it to the group when they meet in class. Each author takes a turn reading his or her paper aloud, while group members follow along silently, taking no more than 10 to 15 minutes each for reading and discussion. Oral reading makes the writer somehow more responsible for his or her expression. Silent reading allows the listeners to mark passages on which to comment once the reading is finished. Five short papers can actually be read and discussed by a disciplined group in 50 minutes—that is, when writers are cautioned not to explain or defend their work, just to take notes.

When students write about events, problems, or situations, and then read their explanations and interpretations to each other, the hour or so that they spend sharing papers is *not* time subtracted from studying or learning, say history, for example. Rather, the students are playing the role of historians, writing and reading history to each other. Writing *about* history—and revising one's writing—is tantamount to thinking about history—and revising that thinking. Time so spent, of course, is time subtracted from being lectured to, but for some teachers the trade-off is well worth it.

QUESTIONS AND ANSWERS ABOUT WORKSHOP CLASSES

What do you need to know about the mechanics of using student groups in class? Following are brief answers to common questions which occur at writing workshops:

1. Are there certain kinds of classes or subjects in which groups work best?

No. From all I have been able to learn, groups of students working together to share ideas or solve problems is as readily useful in a calculus class or biology lab as in history or literature discussion. However, few high school students seem very experienced in collaborative work and so the first efforts may be a bit awkward.

2. Can I use groups in large classes?

Yes and no. I have consistently good results in classes enrolling from 7 to 40 students. Below 7, there really is no need to further subdivide; above 40, it gets difficult to monitor what is going on. However, small groups do provide one good alternative for discussion in very large classes: whereas it is difficult for students to find either time or courage to speak up in a class of 100, many will feel more comfortable talking to ad hoc groups of immediate neighbors.

3. What size group works for what activity?

My experience suggests that groups of three work wonderfully well to solve small problems in a short period of time. I can pose a question to groups of three and have good answers feeding back into the class in 10 minutes. Or such-sized groups can read a paragraph or two to each other and each receive a brief response in about 15 minutes—which means you can do all sorts of other things in the rest of your class. For more interaction or more perspectives on a problem, I use groups of five, but must allow at least 15 to 20 minutes to make sure that each has a chance to have his or her say. Small groups for quick activities; larger groups for more complex ones. If you want a formula for how long a group task should take, allow about four minutes of class time for each person in a group.

4. How do I choose who should go in which groups?

For small quick groups, I suggest that people meet together with those around them—it's fast and convenient. I'd do the same for one-time larger groups, for convenience. But to create permanent groups, I usually count students off by fours, fives, or sixes, depending on the desired number and size of groups. Sometimes I've divided a class into groups to establish a certain female-male mix (believing that mixed groups are more likely to stay on track) or to assure at least one spark plug (and one dullard?) per group. But such deliberate groupings have so often backfired that I've given them up. Simply counting off assures a grouping that breaks up self-selecting class cliques into fresher groups; it is also likely to result in good female-male mixes and seems to promote more harmony because of its randomness.

5. Should I join groups or sit out and do something else?

When I make small open-ended assignments, I join in, which gives the process credibility. But for larger or on-going tasks, I sit

out, wanting the groups to establish a mode of operating independent of me. At such times I usually write in my journal (or
review student journals) and listen casually to what's going on.
I know that my presence *always* skews the process (which you
sometimes want when things aren't working).

6. How can I be sure the groups will stay on task?

One answer is, "You can't." If you want to be sure, you'll
have to sit in all groups at once or appoint observers. However,
short of certitude, there are techniques that deliver great reliability.
I give the problem-solving groups specific tasks to report to the
whole class; either I ask that a secretary take notes or give each
group an overhead projection transparency and request an outline
of their answers or solution. The transparency has proved to be
most effective in such group situations. It provides a lively,
attention-getting means of presenting information to the class.
For on-going writing groups, there is already a very concrete
agenda: reading papers aloud to each other. While first meetings
may not engender much critical feedback, the second and third
times *always get better*.

7. Am I avoiding my responsibility as a teacher if I use groups in
   class?

A loaded question: what you believe about education will tell
you whether or not you are comfortable turning part of a class
over to students. I always trust that student-student discussion
will help learning to go on. True, teachers can use group activity
merely to avoid class preparation, but that will catch up with anyone who attempts it too often. I plan group activity carefully
ahead of time and budget the time tightly. In a 50-minute class,
I may allow 15 minutes for a group problem-solving session, possibly adding a 10-minute whole discussion to explore the results.
That still leaves half the class period for yet another agenda. (There
are times when a class takes off in unpredictable directions, of
course, but it's usually simple enough to hold to a time frame.)
The best way to learn to use groups is to keep trying different
combinations and inventing different tasks, trusting that some are
bound to fail, some to work wonderfully well. Think especially
about your own experiences in small-group situations—about what
seems to work and what doesn't. Don't be afraid to talk over with
your class the elements that are important in small-group work,
especially the importance of listening versus talking.

TRADE-OFFS

A final word on losses and gains. Nothing's free. If you decide to use writing to promote learning in a particular class in the several ways talked about in this book, you will have to do one of two things: either (1) spend more time on that class than you did in the past, or (2) do less of something else in that class than you did before. For most of us the first choice is unacceptable. If writing across the curriculum will mean adding time to your already busy schedule, I would caution about using it: at best, you'll resent the extra time; at worst, you'll stop doing it.

A more reasonable approach is to trade off something else you do as you incorporate more writing. Not in all classes, however. In some classes, where you are completely satisfied with your approach, you won't want to do that; in other classes, where you teach a multiple section from a syllabus shared with other teachers, you won't be able to make your own idiosyncratic modifications; and in still other classes, where you have to cover A, B, and C to prepare students for next semester's D, E, and F, you will have fewer personal choices about what to trade for what. But in all those other classes, where you essentially control how students are introduced to American government or chemistry or art history; or how deeply they investigate the French Revolution or Shakespeare or Newton's Third Law; in all those situations you, the teacher, make choices. You decide how much to cover, where to survey, where to investigate in depth, which and how many books to read, which and how many papers, tests, projects to assign, how best to spend class time, etc. In those situations where you have relative autonomy, that's where to start experimenting with new writing activities. Try one idea in just one small class and see how it goes. Try something else in another and test that too. Use what works, matches your style, suits your needs. Let's conclude by looking at a typical high school or college writing assignment to see how a writing-across-the-curriculum approach might make trade-offs.

THE PROBLEM WITH TERM PAPERS

Suppose you traditionally assign a 10- or 15-page term paper. The teacher time in handling this assignment comes primarily at the end of the term, when you read each paper, carefully critiquing (a) the thesis, (b) the evidence, (c) the style, (d) the conventions, and pointing out how to fix all that's wrong—usually plenty. You may average 45 minutes per paper doing this, after which you affix grades and try to return each paper to its author—some of whom

never pick them up. As far as assignments go, this isn't the best use
of teacher time; in fact, it's rather limited. For one thing, as traditionally assigned, term papers are one-shot productions, where the
writer hands in one draft and considers it done. For another thing,
term papers typically come in at the end of the term so all you
can do is grade them; you can't profitably ask for further revision
of weak arguments or missing information or incorrect assertions.
Finally, there is no formal opportunity for writers to share the
fruits of each other's investigations. In other words, an elaborate
writing assignment that the teacher sees once and the rest of the
class never.

Suppose, instead, that you take that 45 minutes of at-home
evaluation time and redistribute it over the semester in a different
way, but this time, in addition you use three class periods to pay
extra attention to the writing assignment. Such a modification
might look like this: (1) at midterm you ask students to begin
journal writing on possible topics: What do they now know? What
do they want to know? How can they go about finding out? (no
teacher time); (2) soon they generate one-page proposals which
you briefly review overnight and hand back (five minutes teacher
time); (3) next week you give up half a period to an all-class critique of selected revised proposals (no teacher time); (4) a week
later students bring to class three-page first drafts of the papers
and spend one period reading and critiquing each other's drafts
(no teacher time); (5) next week you schedule a 15-minute conference with each writer about a five-page revised second draft
which you review with the student (fifteen minutes teacher time);
(6) two weeks later you schedule brief oral reports on selected research projects (class time; no teacher time); (7) that week you
collect complete second drafts and read each for strength of
argument, paying no attention to editorial matters (10 minutes
teacher time); (8) the week before the final draft is due you appoint editing pairs and ask each to be responsible for editing and
proofing each other's final drafts (no teacher time); (9) next to
last week of class you allow a whole class period for small groups
to read and comment on each other's near-final drafts (class time;
no teacher time; (10) next period you collect and read final
drafts—which you are able to read rapidly because you have
seen them already and because by now they are well written (15
minutes teacher time); (11) the last week of class you return all
papers, highlighting a few and discussing the success (or failure) of
the assignment with the students (class time; no teacher time).

Admittedly, this hypothetical example is more precisely
organized than any multistep process really could be. But you get

the point: by redistributing the time you spend on a weak assignment—*weak* because once handed in the learning for the student is over-you allow the writers to make first drafts and through a process of methodical feedback from both you and fellow students, continue to strengthen both their learning and their writing. You do need to make some trade-offs in class time; the process just described takes about three class periods where you could be doing something else. Consequently, you would want to make sure that the material covered in the project was worth the six or eight weeks during which class attention was focused—to a greater or lesser extent—on the assignment. But the gain is clear: the thinking, the learning, and the expressing become near synonomous and mutually supportive activities. What you trade off in breadth—you may have to cut out one book, unit, or period—you make back in depth: the more complete immersion in the assignment makes for a greater commitment on the part of the learner and a more thorough understanding of the subject.

This is the best example I can think of to demonstrate how the writing begins to affect the quality and quantity of the whole educational experience. It's impossible to remain in didactic mode and effectively complete a process such as I've just described. The trick, of course, is to trust both the writing and the students.

DIDACTIC OBSERVATION

Students talking and writing to each other are the heart of the workshop class. To use such groups as a regular part of your teaching strategy is to tell students that you trust them to contribute meaningful knowledge and insights to your course of instruction. It is my belief that students who experience such instruction regularly do, in fact, learn to take more responsibility for their own learning. The true workshop class encourages writing and reading, talking and listening activities all the time about whatever both students and teacher care about.

WORKSHOP ACTIVITIES

Pre-Chapter Journal Writing

Write for five minutes about each of the following topics:

1. Describe the best teacher you ever had. What made this teacher so special? Or, write about the teacher who most helped you understand writing, helped you like writing; or the reverse, too.
2. Describe yourself as a teacher. What is your main strength?
3. Role-play an average student sitting in one of your classes: how would that student describe one of your typical class periods to a friend?

Post-Chapter Journal Writing

Write for 10 minutes about one of the following topics:

1. In which mode of instruction do you most often find yourself? Explain.
2. Describe modifications you could make in one of your courses to accommodate workshop-style writing assignments.
3. Write about whatever is on your mind right now.

Workshop Exercise

The Helping Circle

A good idea for focusing on selected pieces of student writing is described by Ken Macrorie (1976). The helping circle idea is basically that only when a piece of writing leaves the author's hand and reaches an audience is the circle of communication complete. You can use a helping circle or circles in small classes where you believe that writers would benefit from hearing each others words and ideas. Here are two versions:

1. *The Whole Class.* One writer volunteers to prepare her paper for a whole-class helping circle. She duplicates and distributes copies for the whole group (this works best with 25 or fewer people). The writer reads her paper while the class follows along; she invites comments when she is done. The listeners react to her paper as honestly as possible, paying attention to larger issues of content rather than smaller issues of convention. The teacher, who may act as a leader, tries to maintain a

fair balance in the comments; the writer practices not being defensive. After a class does this once or twice, it becomes comfortable with the supportive purpose of the process.

2. *Small Groups.* Helping circles also work in small groups. Divide a larger class into groups of five, six, or seven and follow the same procedure outlined above. The advantage of the small groups is that more people can read their papers and more people can talk; the disadvantage is that the whole class does not share a common experience. In both groups, some practice makes the process work better (see Guidelines for Responding to Writing, the Classroom Handout which follows; see Macrorie, 1976, for a more complete discussion of this exercise).

Classroom Handout

Guidelines for Responding to Writing

1. *Writers:* Read your paper aloud while the group follows along silently.
2. *Writers:* Take good notes for future revision.
3. *Writers:* Tell your readers what kind of response would help you most.
4. *Writers:* Be open, listen to all suggestions, don't act defensively.
5. *Readers:* Respond honestly to the content of each paper.
6. *Readers:* Respond first to large issues; later to small ones.
7. *Readers:* Put yourself in the writer's shoes and try to be helpful and supportive.
8. *Group:* Budget time so each writer gets a fair hearing.
9. *Group:* Stick closely to the paper and subject of the paper.
10. *Group:* Be aware that good talkers are first good listeners.
11. *Group:* If any writer is short-changed on time, give written responses and rotate the starting order next time you meet.
12. *Group:* Keep all writing in a portfolio, including drafts; give me a copy of the paper you read each time.

Note: Good books to consult about responding to writers include those by Peter Elbow (1973, 1981) and Ken Macrorie (1984, 1985).

Teachers Respond

Evaluating the Writing Workshop

1.   The feeling of exhilaration is a little worn off by now—I'm tired! And feel somewhat brain-drained! I want to move away from this for a short while so that I can look at it anew with a fresh mind. But I know I am changed from this—more determined, more convinced that all this may *really* be possible to implement—and not just educational bureaucratic jargon. I learned more from this workshop about thinking. . . . Is that because I did a lot of writing . . . ???

2.   To me, this workshop is characterized mostly by *experiencing* rather than *talking about* writing. Why? We all came to the workshop, presumably, because we already think student writing is important. If asked to give reasons, we'd probably say things like how important it will be in students' futures . . . , or . . . how students must do a better job of communicating with us. . . .

Writing is thinking, writing is learning. . . . To convince us that writing belongs at the center of a university curriculum . . . is to let us experience its power. (And satisfaction.)

And so we write. We stumble on insights; we remember stuff from the past, we enjoy writing. For me, all of those are important, but perhaps the last is the most important of all. If we rediscover the pleasures of unevaluated writing, writing for teaching the self, we'll want that for students as well.

3.   This has been really fascinating. As a music teacher, I have always been interested in different ways that we express ourselves. I have always been a supporter of writing (and an avid reader) but didn't have or take the time to "put it together" in my classes. The idea that writing facilitates thinking should have been more obvious to me. Now I have both better justification and tools to use writing in my classes.

4.   When I opened my "first day of workshop" proposed program and read the synopsis for the first day, I thought, boy what has this to do with me? I teach math. However, I see some real possibilities with thinking-writing process for problem solving. Math can be at times dull—I'm always looking for ways to vary my teaching method—this helps.

References

American Association for the Advancement of the Humanities. (1982, February). Analysts: Schools. *Humanities Report 4*(2).

Applebee, A. N. (1981). *Writing in the secondary school. English and the content areas* (NCTE Research Report No. 21). Urbana, IL: National Council of Teachers of English.

Bailey, R. (1983). Writing across the curriculum — the British approach. In P. L. Stock (Ed.), *Fforum: Essays on theory and practice in the teaching of writing.* Montclair, NJ: Boynton/Cook.

Bennett, W. J. (1984). *To reclaim a legacy: A report on the humanities in higher education.* Washington, DC: U.S. Government Printing Office.

Berthoff, A. E. (1978). *Forming/thinking/writing: The composing imagination.* Rochelle Park, NJ: Hayden.

Britton, J. (1970). *Language and learning.* New York: Penguin.

Britton, J. (1982). Writing to learn and learning to write. In G. M. Pradl (Ed.), *Prospect and retrospect: Selected essays of James Britton.* Montclair, NJ: Boynton/Cook.

Britton, J. (1983). Language and learning across the curriculum. In P. L. Stock (Ed.), *Fforum: Essays on theory and practice in the teaching of writing.* Montclair, NJ: Boynton/Cook.

Britton, J., et al. (1975). *The development of writing abilities (11-18).* London: Macmillan.

Coles, W. E., Jr. (1983). The literacy crisis: A challenge how? In P. L. Stock (Ed.), *Fforum: Essays on theory and practice in the teaching of writing.* Montclair, NJ: Boynton/Cook.

D'Angelo, F. J. (1983). Imitation and the teaching of style. In P. L. Stock (Ed.), *Fforum: Essays on theory and practice in the teaching of writing.* Montclair, NJ: Boynton/Cook.

Elbow, P. (1973). *Writing without teachers.* New York: Oxford University Press.

Elbow, P. (1981). *Writing with power.* New York: Oxford University Press.

Elbow, P. (1983). Teaching writing by not paying attention to writing. In P. L. Stock (ED.), *Fforum: Essays on theory and practice in the teaching of writing.* Montclair, NJ: Boynton/Cook.

Emig, J. (1978). Hand, eye, brain: Some "basics" in the writing process. In C. R. Cooper & L. Odell (Eds.), *Research on composing: Points of departure.* Urbana, IL: National Council of Teachers of English.

Emig, J. (1977, May). Writing as a mode of learning. *College Composition and Communication, 28,* 122–128.

Fader, D. (1966). *Hooked on books.* New York: Medallion.

Faigley, L. & T. P. Miller (1982, October). What we learn from writing on the job. *College English, 44*(6), 557–569.

Flower, L. (1979, September). Writer-based prose: A cognitive basis for problems in writing. *College English, 41,* 19–37.

Flower, L. (1981). *Problem solving strategies for writing.* New York: Harcourt Brace Jovanovich.

Flower, L. & J. R. Hayes (1981, December). A cognitive process theory of writing. *College Composition and Communication, 32,* 365–387.

Freire, P. (1970). *Pedagogy of the oppressed.* New York: Herder and Herder.

Freisinger, R. (1980, Winter/Spring). James Britton and the importance of audience. *English Language Arts Bulletin, 20/21,* 5–8.

Freisinger, R. (1982). Cross-disciplinary writing programs: Beginnings. In T. Fulwiler & A. Young (Eds.), *Language connections: Writing and reading across the curriculum.* Urbana, IL: National Council of Teachers of English.

Fulwiler, T. (1981, January). Showing, not telling at a faculty workshop. *College English, 43,* 55–63.

Fulwiler, T. (in press). How well does writing across the curriculum work. *College English.*

Gibson, W. (1969). *Persona.* New York: Random House.

Goodman, K. S. (1968). *The psycholinguistic nature of the reading process.* Detroit: Wayne State University Press.

Goswami, D., J. C. Redish, D. B. Felker, & A. Siegel (1981). *Writing in the professions.* Washington, DC: American Institutes for Research.

Graves, D. (1978). *Balance the basics: Let them write.* New York: The Ford Foundation.

Gusdorf, G. (1977). Speaking as encounter. In M. Nystrand (Ed.), *Language as a way of knowing: A book of readings.* Toronto: The Ontario Institute for Studies in Education.

Johnson, G. (1981, September). *Writing Across the Disciplines Newsletter, 1* (1).

Langer, S. (1960). *Philosophy in a new key* (3rd ed.). Cambridge, MA: Harvard University Press.

Lanham, R. (1979). *Revising prose.* New York: Scribner's.

Macrorie, K. (1980). *Searching writing.* Rochelle Park, NJ: Hayden.

Macrorie, K. (1984). *Writing to be read* (3rd ed.). Upper Montclair, NJ: Boynton/Cook.

Macrorie, K. (1985). *Telling writing* (4th ed.). Upper Montclair, NJ: Boynton/Cook.

Martin, N., P. D'Arcy, B. Newton, & R. Parker (1976). *Writing and learning across the curriculum (11–16).* London: Ward Lock.

McClellan, J. (1978, November). A clinic for misspellers. *College English, 40*(3), 324–329.

McCrimmon, J. (1976). Writing as a way of knowing. In R. Graves (Ed.), *Rhetoric and composition: A sourcebook for teachers and writers* (New ed.). Upper Montclair, NJ: Boynton/Cook.

McLuhan, M. (1964). *Understanding media: The extensions of man.* New York: McGraw-Hill.

Meiland, J. (1983). Methods of thinking and college education. In P. L. Stock (Ed.), *Fforum: Essays on theory and practice in the teaching of writing.* Montclair, NJ: Boynton/Cook.

Moffett, J. (1968). *Teaching the universe of discourse.* Boston: Houghton Mifflin.

Moffett, J. (1981). *Active voice: A writing program across the curriculum.* Montclair, NJ: Boynton/Cook.

Moffett, J. (1982, March). Writing, inner speech, and meditation. *College English, 44(3),* 231–246.

Murray, D. (1978). Internal revision: A process of discovery. In C. R. Cooper & L. Odell (Eds.), *Research on composing: Points of departure.* Urbana, IL: National Council of Teachers of English.

Murray, D. (1980). Writing as process: How writing finds its own meaning. In T. R. Donovan & B. W. McClelland (Eds.), *Eight approaches to teaching composition.* Urbana, IL: National Council of Teachers of English.

Nystrand, M. (Ed.). (1977). *Language as a way of knowing: A book of readings.* Toronto: The Ontario Institute for Studies in Education.

Odell, L. (1980, February). The process of writing and the process of learning. *College Composition and Communication, 32,* 42–50.

Odell, L. (1983). How English teachers can help their colleagues teach writing. In P. L. Stock (Ed.), *Fforum: Essays on theory and practice in the teaching of writing.* Montclair, NJ: Boynton/Cook.

Ohmann, R. (1976). *English in America: A radical view of the profession.* New York: Oxford University Press.

Perl, S. (1979). Unskilled writers as composers. *New York University Education Quarterly, 10,* 17–25.

Rennert, R. A. (1975). Values clarification, journals, and the freshman writing course. In O. H. Clapp (Ed.), *On righting writing.* Urbana, IL: National Council of Teachers of English.

Shaughnessy, M. (1977). *Errors and expectations.* New York: Oxford University Press.

Smith, F. (1971). *Understanding reading: A psycholinguistic analysis of reading and learning to read.* New York: Holt, Rinehart and Winston.

Sommers, N. (1980, December). Revision strategies of student writers and experienced adult writers. *College Composition and Communication, 31,* 378–388.

Stinson, R. (1980, Spring). Journals in the geography class. *WLA Newsletter,* 15.

Strunk, W., & E. B. White. (1979). *The elements of style* (3rd ed.). New York: Macmillan.

U.S. Department of Education & National Commission on Excellence in Education (1983). *A nation at risk: The imperative for educational reform.* Washington, DC: U.S. Government Printing Office.

U.S. Department of Education & National Institute of Education Study Group on the Conditions of Excellence in Higher Education (1984). *Involvement in learning: Realizing the potential of American higher education.* Washington, DC: U.S. Government Printing Office.

Vygotsky, L. S. (1962). *Thought and language.* Cambridge, MA: MIT Press.

Watson, M. (1980, October). Writing in math class. *Mathematics Teacher,* 518–519

Young, A. (1983). Value and purpose in writing. In P. L. Stock (Ed.), *Fforum: Essays in theory and practice in the teaching of writing.* Montclair, NJ: Boynton/Cook.

Ziegler, A. (1981). *The writing workshop* (Vol. 1). New York: Teachers and Writers Collaborative.

Zinsser, W. (1980). *On writing well: An informal guide to writing non-fiction* (2nd ed.). New York: Harper & Row.